Items should be returned on or before the last date
shown below. Items not already requested by other
borrowers may be renewed in person, in writing or by
telephone. To renew, please quote the number on the
barcode label. To renew online a PIN is required.
This can be requested at your local library.
Renew online @ **www.dublincitypubliclibraries.ie**
Fines charged for overdue items will include postage
incurred in recovery. Damage to or loss of items will
be charged to the borrower.

Leabharlanna Poiblí Chathair Bhaile Átha Cliath
Dublin City Public Libraries

Dublin City
Baile Átha Cliath

Coolock Branch Tel: 8477781

Date Due	Date Due	Date Due
07 APR 10.		
22. APR 10.		
20. JUN 1		
19.6.13.		

The Streets of

WEXFORD

Nicky Rossiter

This book is for Ellie, Finn, Lola and Ziggy,
hoping one of you might continue the interest and the work.

The author's royalties will go to
The Tracie Lawlor Trust for Cystic Fibrosis.

First published 2009

Nonsuch Ireland
119 Lower Baggot Street,
Dublin 2
www.nonsuchireland.com

© Nicky Rossiter, 2009

ISBN 978 184588 959 3

Typesetting and origination by The History Press
Printed in Great Britain

Contents

Introduction

Do you remember back in your school days when you wrote your address on your books? It went something like this,

Nicholas Rossiter
23 Bishopswater
Bride Street Parish
Wexford
Ireland
The British Isles
Europe
The World
The Universe
The Solar System

We all wanted to pinpoint our place. Apart from the most intimate sense of place of family and home, the street is our real reference point (or it may be the townland for rural dwellers).

The street defined friendships, loyalties, and often boundaries. In earlier times people often confined interaction to their streets or neighbourhoods. In these streets and neighbourhoods there were also intense rivalries – not always confined to the sports fields.

The word 'street' comes from the Latin 'strata', and in the Middle Ages the word came to denote the main thoroughfare in a town or village. It is interesting to note that in a publicity handout that I received for a recent television programme it was stated that 300 years ago – around the early 1700s – Liverpool was classed as a 'seven-street town'.

Quoted in *Hore's History of Wexford Town and County*, we find that the suburbs of Wexford in 1659 were classed as: Faigh (the Faythe); Bridstreete (Bride Street); St John Streete (John Street); Weststreete (Westgate), and Maudlintown. This gives some indication of the streets existing at the time. To these would have been added the core streets like Main Street, High Street, etc.

In Pigot's Directory of 1820 the street addresses listed are: Back, Main, Selskar, John, Cornmarket, Slaney, Westgate, Old Pound, Common Quay, Faith, Custom House Quay, Bullring, Castle, Monck, Anne, Mary, Ram, Paul Quay, Stonebridge, and George.

While researching this book I had to decide some terms of reference and in particular what to leave out. The primary decisions were that lanes would be excluded (these are covered extensively in *The Journal of The Wexford Historical Society, Volume 19*), that Main Street North and South would be left to a future survey of their own, and that newer streets (often with little connection other than to a species of tree favoured by a developer) would be left out. In general I chose streets extant in Griffith's Valuation (*c.*1854) plus a few others that are interesting in their own right. If yours is missing, I apologise.

I am indebted to Dominic Kiernan who generously provided so many of the exclusive photographs that enhance this publication and was so informative about the people and places depicted.

Thanks once more to Anne for the love, support and the patience.

I hope you will enjoy this excursion into the past. As always I welcome any comments, extra tales or pictures of Wexford's past, and you can share them with me via email at stories@iol.ie.

Abbey Street

Origins and Meanings

Abbey Street, like streets of the same name in other towns throughout the world, takes its name from a nearby abbey. In this case it is from Selskar Abbey, one of the first Wexford churches dating to before the Norman invasion.

Earliest Mentions

In the thirteenth century there was mention of Market Street, which could have been an early reference to this street leading from the Cornmarket. This is mentioned in Hore and also by Dr Hadden in his articles on the development of Wexford:

> We must assume the existence of a high-level connecting trail where Abbey Street now runs, giving access at all times from the Market Place to the never-flooding Causeway when spring tides were covering the more direct beach trail (today's Lower Main Street to the Ferry). Such must have been the outline when in 1300 the Normans extended the Wall to include the Township.

Abbey Street is noted as Lower Back Street in a map drawn from data at the time of the Cromwellian campaign in 1649.

In a map of 1800 it is called Selskar Street.

In 1812 the name is Lower Back Street. This probably came about because of a connection to Back Street, now Mallin Street.

On a map dated 1845 the name Abbey Street has been appended.

Buildings

One of the oldest structures on Abbey Street is the town wall and tower. The tower has been refurbished and it was at its base in 1982 that the official twinning ceremony of Wexford and Coeuron took place.

Joe Murphy's forge was near the tower, which you can still see between The Arts Centre and the houses, back when the street was a much more mixed development. Prior to the mid-twentieth century the street had houses, workshops, animals and every other necessity.

The Central Constabulary Barracks was at the north-east corner with Georges Street. It later became a girls' school. This was Miss Beirne's Girls' School, built by Madame Hatton of Clonard, who also owned Great Clonard and Little Clonard and was a sister of Lord Castlereagh of the Union. The garden of the school extended most of the way down to the back of the houses on the Main Street.

Many people will recall Fran Moran's shop on that corner – 'The Gem'. It was

The milk is delivered on Abbey Street by horse and cart, via tilley can and jug. It was obviously a busy time, with two delivery men active. (*Dominic Kiernan Collection.*)

Abbey Street from Cornmarket. (*Dominic Kiernan Collection.*)

there you stocked up on goodies for the pictures before going to the Abbey Cinema in George Street.

A boys' boarding school was recorded in Abbey Street in 1824. This may have been John Kiely's, where, it was noted in 1826, he charged 3s 7d per week boarding. The school recorded twenty-four Roman Catholic and eleven Protestant pupils in 1826.

The Protestant infant school was located at 44 Abbey Street in 1853. This is the only school mentioned in the street in Griffith's Valuation.

The older houses, including the one housing the doctor's surgery in Abbey Street, are believed to date from between 1815 and 1835.

An advertisement from 1872 reads: 'Patrick Kehoe, The General Posting Establishment, Abbey Street informs his friends and the public that he has for hire several well-appointed Cars, inside and outside, which he will let on moderate terms. A trial will convince.'

In the twentieth century White's Hotel was redeveloped and fronted on to Abbey Street. There they had The Shelmelier Bar and a lovely big foyer where a blazing fire welcomed the winter crowds. The County Council later used it as a library with the children's section located in the old restaurant and the adult books in the old bar with its grand fireplace. The books were stamped for lending at what had been the old reception desk. History repeated itself in the early twenty-first century, when White's Hotel once again faced on to Abbey Street following a major rebuilding programme.

Davy Tobin's was a fixture on the north-west corner of Abbey Street and Georges Street in the late 1900s. Mr Tobin did not own the business (it was part of Coffey's, whose main shop was on South Main Street) but it always went by his name among true Wexford natives. It was in this pawnbroker's that many a good suit spent its weekdays, only to be redeemed on the Saturday afternoon to be brushed off and ready for Mass on Sunday. Pawnbrokers were the welfare service and banks of their day for the poorer people of every town. Today we casually forget how difficult times were half a century ago. If you were out of work you did not eat and worse still your family didn't. To get so-called relief you would be quizzed as to why you should get help. Charities like the St Vincent de Paul Society did what they could, but the Wexford and Ireland of that era was a far cry from the Celtic Tiger.

Abbey Street and Howlin's Barbershop. (*Dominic Kiernan Collection.*)

Abbey Street. The entrance to Coffey's Pawnshop, better known as Davy Tobin's. (*Dominic Kiernan Collection.*)

Sister Phillip on Abbey Street. The black door opposite her is the entrance to Mucky Moran's scrapyard in Abbey Street. Next to that, on the right, was Miss Roche's. A retired nurse, she used to collect accounts for Sloan's and other stores. On the right of the entrance was 'Dandy' Dan Doyle's and out of view, on the left was the home of 'Danno' Murphy.

Wages for those lucky enough to be in work were small and seldom stretched to the week's end. This sparked the vicious circle of pawning the suit or other valuables – not the family jewels, few had anything of much worth – to get cash to buy food on Monday or Tuesday. Then, when payday came on Friday, the items were redeemed with a small commission going to the pawnbroker. But this took more out of the wages that week, so the money ran out quicker and the items had to be pawned again.

People tend to think that life was easier in the time of their parents and grandparents. It was in some ways, but who among you could juggle that sort of life week in and week out? They also feel that our ancestors were less financially astute. They did not use banks or credit cards but they had to negotiate a myriad of financial schemes, from tontine to club money to pawnbrokers to shopkeeper loans and food on tick.

In Griffith's Valuation the landowners include: John A. Hogan; reps of John Carty; John Stafford; David Robinson; John Sparrow; John Kinsella; reps of James Percival; Sarah Hamilton; Mark Devereux; Anne Massey; Henry Mullen; reps of Thomas Redmond; Robert Anglin; John E. Hadden; Eliza Delamour; Ellen Hayes, and Charles Bell.

People and Events

Eliza Gainfort had a shop on North Main Street.

One Wexford seaman who earned distinction was Henry Mullen of Abbey Street. While serving on the British ship *Trabolgan* he gave assistance to a Spanish ship found on fire in the Atlantic. In recognition of this act, Queen Isabella of Spain had a special medal struck for the Wexfordman.

John Roberts, sometime Clerk of the Peace for the County of Wexford died in Abbey Street in 1834.

The Harbour Constable in 1914 was Andrew Sinnott of Abbey Street, and he was appointed to carry out duties on Sundays.

When excavations were carried out in the area in 1976, the so-called Abbey Street Pottery was found to date to the period 1650-1750.

James Furlong, rate collector, bought two houses in Abbey Street for £60.

In a newspaper interview in the early twenty-first century John Wilson recalled his days delivering coal in Wexford, 'When we delivered around Cornmarket and Abbey Street, there were still half-doors on the houses. You don't see them anymore.'

Allen Street facing towards Main Street with Ward's grocery visible where Hore's now stands. The building on the right with curved windows was probably the Methodist Hall referred to in the text. (*Dominic Kiernan Collection.*)

Allen Street from the direction of Main Street. (*Dominic Kiernan Collection.*)

Allen Street

Origins and Meaning

Allen Street is named after the Revd Joseph Allen who owned a large part of the area. In Griffith's Valuation, Joseph Allen owned eight of the eleven properties listed.

It was opened as a street in 1793 and paved by Corporation that year. In the Corporation minutes of June 1793 it was referred to as 'the new street opened by Robert Allen'.

The Allen brothers, Richard, Maurice and Robert were major forces in our maritime history. Their trade extended to four continents from offices near the present North Station. Most of their vessels were built in Canada and their business was largely in the fruit and grain trades, Galati (formerly Galatz) in Romania being one of their destinations. Their barque *Wexford*, which was bought in 1851 and weighed 307 tons, carried emigrants to Savannah and New Orleans, returning with cotton for Liverpool. A captain Codd commanded her.

Other Allen ships were: *Forth*, a 200 tonner; *Selskar*, of eighty-one tons; *Menapia*; *Esperia*; *Rapid*; a schooner called *Annie* skippered by 'Big Ned Reilly', and another called *Spray* under the command of Jemmy Storey. The Allens' *Saltee* sailed to Canada regularly for timber.

Earliest Mentions

It was known as Broad Street in 1649.

In the map of 1800 it has attained the name Allen Street.

Buildings

Corbett & Rochford Ladies' Boarding School was located here in 1824. It was also referred to as Miss Rochfort's. In a list of 1826 Miss Rochfort's is shown housing forty-nine Roman Catholic and one other denomination pupil. The weekly fee was 10*d*.

The post office was in Allen Street in 1824.

There was a Methodist church here in the eighteenth century.

People and Events

In 1824 John Hickey was postmaster and during his tenure the mail from Dublin arrived at 10.15a.m. and from Munster and England at 1.30p.m.

In an 1823 newspaper we find a notice, 'Sermon in Methodist Chapel at 7p.m., collection for home and foreign missions.'

An advertisement in 1823 announced a musical event on the street, 'In Assembly Rooms by Mr Panormo of Dublin. He will perform pieces on grand pianoforte, which he offers for sale at a reduced price. Admission 4*d* & 2*d*, tickets from himself at Mr Campbell's, Allen Street.'

The Trade Union Movement secured the co-operation of every tradesman in the town in 1843 with the result that the committee were able to establish their headquarters in Allen Street, in a house that had up to then been used by the Methodists as a chapel. The Methodists vacated the premises on the completion of their chapel in Rowe Street.

In the early days of Pierce's foundry the castings may have come from Donnelley's in Allen Street. The first cast-iron product made by James Pierce at his new premises in Allen Street in 1839 was a simple fire fan or fire machine.

In 1911, Stephen Joseph Howlin lived at 3 Allen Street.

A commendation for gallant conduct was bestowed on Lance Corporal Michael O'Connor of Allen Street when he was aged eighteen years. O'Connor served in the 16th Division of the Irish Brigade in 1917.

In byelaws of 1955, parking was prohibited in Allen Street.

Anne Street

Origins and Meaning
Anne Street most probably takes its name from Queen Anne (1665-1714), although the first use of the name is to be found long after her reign. On maps drawn from data of 1649 and the town plan of 1800, a street or lane is depicted but is not named.

The official name was changed to Thomas Ashe Street by a Borough Council decision of 1 September 1920. In 1932 a plebiscite was taken to legalise this decision but it was not passed and the change could not be legalised. A further decision to make the alteration was made in 1981.

Earliest Mentions
Up to 1700 there was probably a steep cliff falling to the harbour at this point.

At one time it was called Headland Lane.

The upper section of the street was built up before 1812. It was called Shambles Street, the shambles (meat market) having moved from The Bullring in the 1700s. The shambles was located in a lane running parallel to the present street. It was known as The Flesh Market around 1800.

The major construction of the quays led to the development of the seaward section of Anne Street.

Buildings
The Georgian houses appear to have been built in three blocks. Of these, most of the lower block on the south side was taken over in 1828 by the Harbour Commissioners as the Ballast Office and later by Inland Revenue as offices. Both houses were taken over as clubs, the lower by the Free Masons and the other by Wexford Club, to be succeeded in the twentieth century by the Labour Exchange, and the National Club.

'Meeting of Wexford Harbour Commissioners on 6 January 1857 at the Ballast

Anne Street, prior to the major changes of the late 1900s. On the extreme left is the hall where 'pongo' was played. McCormack's was on the site of the original 'Labour Exchange'. The County Hotel dominates the right side. (*Rossiter Collection.*)

Office, Anne Street, Wexford. The salary of Patrick O'Connor from 30 September to 31 December as Superintendent of Ballast and Ballast Lighter was set as £7-10-0.'

The older section of Wexford Credit Union was purpose-built by Bresleau Brothers, contractors, as a branch office of the Provincial Bank of Ireland.

Up the street, in the upper of the two houses, was born Harry Furniss, the famous Punch cartoonist, son of the manager of the Wexford Gas Co.

The Racquetball court was the second building from the corner on the south side.

Mr William Powell first opened the Bonded Stores in Anne Street in 1835. The Wexford Bonding Store was still here in 1902. This was almost opposite the present post office and John E. Sinnott recalled a great apple tree in the yard.

Hopkins and Busher had a garage in Anne Street where they ran hackney cars.

The Methodist church was built in 1836. Thomas Willis, a local architect, designed it.

The General post office was built in 1894. On 15 May 1895 Edward Solly Flood noted in his diary, 'Drove to Wexford for Petty Sessions. Walked to the new post office in Anne Street.'

Number 8 Anne Street housed Anglim's. They were the printers of the *Wexford Illustrated Almanac*.

Jem Murphy owned a ship called the *Economist*, so called because it was designed to require no ballast, thus reducing its running costs. Murphy was also a publican and owned what was later to become 'The Shamrock Bar' in Anne Street, a pub much favoured by seafarers.

The Shamrock Hotel of 1885 became 'The Shamrock Bar'. It was also once known as 'Foxe's' and was owned by P. Meyler by 1945. Pierce Roche later owned it and it finds literary immortality in the novel *Tumbling Down*, written by his son Billy.

Clancy's Hotel was originally a house owned by Clancy, a victualler. He operated a butcher's shop in the porch of the hotel. It became 'The County Hotel' when sold in June 1947 to Sinnott's. There was once a lane beside the hotel where Mamie Scanlon had a furniture store.

In 1853, No.3a was a slaughterhouse, No.9 was the Custom House, and No.17 the Presbyterian church.

Thomas and Mathew Boggan opened a garage in 1920s and ran a bus fleet from Anne Street. *Banshee* and *Bluebird* were the names of two of their buses. They also operated a parcel delivery service along the routes.

Lamb House, owned by Con Collins, was located at the top south side of Anne Street. It was here that Dunnes Stores originally opened in Wexford.

Pongo sessions were run in a store near the top of Anne Street called 'Knoxie's'.

In Griffith's Valuation there are notes on a slaughterhouse, the custom house and the Presbyterian meeting house. The primary landowners are named as Charles and Ebenezer Jacobs and Robert Hughes. Martin Murphy owned one piece of the street. The Corporation of Wexford owned the Bonding Store.

People and Events

The Georgians built vaults on which to support the roadway, curving it towards the top so that a gentler slope was obtained. The line of the upper end of the road ensured that horses drew their coaches across the slope as they rounded the corner at the top. Anne Street was designed as the central traffic link between the new thoroughfare of the quay and the new business area of the Main Street.

In 1817 this advertisement appeared, 'Mr Garbois, professor of dancing, informs nobility and gentry that he will give instruction twice a month. All the new Quadrilles and Cotillions, waltzing, *pas seuls* and fancy figures taught. Apply Miss O'Brien's Boarding School, Anne Street.'

In 1823, eight boxes of Mauld candles and five hogsheads tobacco were advertised for auction at Matthew Devereux's in Anne Street.

An 1823 notice: 'An English establishment for the sale of woollen goods will be opened at the shop and ware-rooms attached to the house of Mr James Barry, Main Street, near Anne Street. Will sell for ready money only.'

In 1824 John Sutherland is listed as owning a hotel in Anne Street.

James Furniss of Anne Street founded the Gasworks in 1830. It went bankrupt in 1865 and was replaced by a new company.

Clement Archer lived at Anne Street in 1834 and may have owned the land of Archer's Lane.

Fr Mathew was in Wexford on 8 April 1841. A Temperance Crusade began at The Friary on 10 April 1841 and thousands attended. A room at Clancy's Hotel in Anne Street was let to the Temperance Club in 1850. It was the first popular reading room in Wexford. It charged a subscription of 1*d* per week. The Temperance Society started here before moving to its own hall at Temperance Row.

English's Printing Works opened at corner of Anne Street in 1883. It specialised in high-class printing and handcrafted bookbinding. The firm also supplied and manufactured ledger books to local business houses such as Walker's, Godkin's, Frank O'Connor's Bakery, Philip Pierce, and the Star Engineering Works. College annuals were also printed and bound for Rockwell, Blackrock, Mungret and St Peter's College, as well as numerous periodicals. The famous *Capuchin Annual* was one of English's most prestigious publications. Wexford Festival Opera programme was another product of the English printing presses. The diocesan catechisms, small and large versions, were also printed in Anne Street. Family names such as Scallan, O'Leary, Donnelly, O'Grady, Dempsey, Hogan, Kinsella, Busher and Sinnott played a major role in the everyday workings of the firm. Mr English was an imposing figure who always wore a suit and bow tie. He had a summerhouse in the Windmill Hills near Wygram where he and his wife sojourned from June to September every year, commuting from Wygram to Anne Street on a daily basis.

In 1914 Llewelyn Morgan of Anne Street was working as a motor engineer.

In August 1925 the estimated cost of resurfacing Anne Street was £10 8*s* 0*d*.

In December of the same year there was a letter from N. Lambert and J. Sinnott requesting permission to open Anne Street in order to lay water pipes and extend the entrance to Lambert's Bakery. Permission was granted provided the road was restored to its previous condition afterwards.

Excavations in 1963 at lower Anne Street uncovered a 12-14ft depth of sandy beach.

In 1939 the Corporation discussed the parking of cars in the horse and cart tracks on Anne Street, causing the carts to have to use the middle of the road. These tracks were specifically provided to allow horses to negotiate the upper part of the street.

The School of Wireless Telegraphy in 1914 invited young men of seventeen to twenty-four years to train as operators. For terms, they were to apply to the Principal, Anne Street.

Other

The mail coach, on leaving the stables in Selskar near the Priory Gate, descended Trimmer's Lane to the post office on the quay to pick up the mail. It then went up Anne Street to the Coach Office at No. 3 North Main Street, and along to White's Hotel for more passengers before hitting the open road.

Back Street

Origins and Meaning

In Medieval towns, the principal street was usually named 'High' or 'Fore' Street, with Back Street to its rear, hence the British term 'high-street stores'. Wexford confused matters by calling the street that continued on from High Street, Back Street. Today we officially call it Mallin Street, commemorating one of the Irish patriots. This decision was made in 1920 and legalised by plebiscite in 1932.

Earliest Mentions

In a reference in 1680 regarding to soldiers who served Cromwell, the following is noted about the area, 'an additional building backwards slated, a courtledge, a shed and stable slated, a yard and slated sheds in it, with a key to the river, in the Marketplace, all in Back-street, town of Wexford.'

From an Inquisition of August 1697 it appears that Patrick Murphy was the tenant of 'a thatched Mass House in Back Street'.

Back Street was called Cornmarket Street in 1772.

In 1764 there was a mention of Back Street.

Pigot's Directory notes Back Street in 1820.

Buildings

Most Revd Dr Sweetman was parish priest of Wexford from 1736 to 1745. After his consecration as Bishop of Ferns he continued to act as Pastor until 1756. In 1743 he lodged with John Murphy, a shopkeeper, in Back Street, and had Fr Walsh as his assistant.

There was a printer in Back Street also, and in 1782 George Lyneall printed the *Wexford Chronicle* here.

In 1808 an advert appeared in the *Wexford Herald*, 'To be let – Brewery concerns and dwelling house in Back Street now occupied by Laurence and John Murphy. The copper with a capacity of thirty barrels is good as new. It has perfect command of excellent water.'

In 1824 Michael M. Quinn had a pawnbroker shop and Miss Rochford had a school in Back Street.

A list for 1826 shows that Joe and Charlotte Browne had a school with twenty pupils here, charging fees of 2½d per week. Michael Donnolly also had a school in Back Street in 1826, housing thirty-two Roman Catholic and twelve other denomination pupils at 6¼d per week.

In more recent history many will recall the back entrance for Godkin's opening out on to the street. In those stores they had not just provisions for the shop on the Main Street, but also tons of various meals and seeds for farmers. Here the farmers of the twentieth century came to buy grain beside where the farmers of the 1300s came to sell their grains.

According to Griffith the major landowners on Back Street included Hayes, Kenny, Doran, Hatchell, Allen, Taylor, Harpur, Walsh, Whitney, Prendergast, Tottenham and Guilfoyle.

People and Events

In 1809 a fire in Back Street at the corn store of Richard Stafford consumed a store and dwelling house, as well as the adjoining house, which belonged to Thomas Gregory, a brewer. We presume he is the one who bought the aforementioned brewery. The thatched building burned down despite the best efforts of all, including members of the Kilkenny Militia and the mayor. Water had to be carried some distance. According to the *Wexford Herald*, sparks fell on a smith's forge some distance away and it burned so quickly that even the bellows was lost.

Other

Neville's Entry once connected the Main Street and Back Street.

Barrack Street

Origins and Meaning

Barrack Street takes its name from the military barracks that take up a large portion of the street.

The official name is Macken Street, as designated by the Borough Council on 1 September 1920. In 1932 a plebiscite was taken to legalise this decision but it was not passed and the change could not be legalised. A further decision was made in 1981 to make the alteration.

Earliest Mentions

The Military Barracks is possibly on the site of an original fortification built by the Norse. Water is said to have lapped at the base prior to major land reclamation in the eighteenth century. Until the seventeenth century it was said to have been a four-tower castle like the Tower of London, with its own fresh-water well. Following the demolition of that building in 1725, the present one was erected and it remains one of the earliest surviving purpose-built civic institutions in the area.

In 1812 the Barracks (or Castle as it was then called) was listed as a gaol.

There was a Constabulary Barracks in 1880 at the corner of Barrack Street, where the post office now stands.

Mr Wm Murphy bought Miss Browne's pipe factory at the King Street end of Barrack Street in around 1889.

Buildings

Some of the houses in Barrack Street, such as No.11, are thought to date from between 1790 and 1810.

The Military Barracks was consecrated to the Sacred Heart in October 1922.

Barrack Street preparing for one of the many processions held each year. The pub on the left was Beakey's. (*Dominic Kiernan Collection.*)

The Military Barracks was fired on in 1922 from a field near Distillery Road, probably behind the CBS. Over twenty rounds were fired but there was no return fire. Some of the bullets were found lodged in the walls of Mr W. Murphy's bedroom in Barrack Street.

One of the most popular buildings in Wexford – as far as young people were concerned – was Maggie Kelly's in Barrack Street. As well as groceries she carried a wide range of cheap toys and of particular interest were 'the parcels'. These were pre-wrapped packages containing a variety of trinkets and novelties.

In Griffith's Valuation the major portion of Barrack Street is owned by John E. Redmond with other owners listed as: Bailey; John White; Edmund Hore; Richard Burke; Joseph Meadows; Dutton and Mary White; William Neville; William Furlong, and Patrick Furlong, with some 'waste building ground' owned by Gibson, Buchanan and Richards.

People and Events

On 16 April 1798 the North Cork Militia moved into the Barracks at Wexford with their wives and children.

Private Abbott shot himself while on gate duty at the Barracks on 26 September 1834.

On 20 August 1894, Edward Solly Flood wrote in his diary, 'James Redmond of Barrack Street came and examined ceiling of dining room. He agreed that there would be no use patching it, the whole ceiling must be renewed.' Redmond, builder of Barrack Street, is mentioned in Bassett.

The Wexford Militia were recruiting in 1896, offering, '8d daily pocket money, three good meals a day, butter and jam always for breakfast, meat dinner with vegetables. Good pair of boots, shirt and socks to take home. 2/- for bringing in new blood – Apply Barracks.'

In 1902 J.J. Perceval, secretary of Wexford Loan Fund Society, summoned James Meyler of Barrack Street for the sum of 4s 9d. Also Margaret Anne Hutchinson, shopkeeper, sued Patrick and Mary Malone, Barrack Street for 17s owed since November 1901.

At Christmas in 1903 in the Military Barracks, the non-commissioned officers of the 3rd Royal Irish Regiment had their annual smoking concert on St Stephen's Night, 'A most enjoyable night of music and song was spent over the burning of the 'soothing weed'. A feature was the gramophone exhibition given by Mr C.E. Vize. A most enjoyable smoker was brought to a successful close at midnight.'

In September 1914, the Postmaster asked for Corporation permission to close post offices at Barrack Street and North Main Street at 7.30p.m. instead of 8p.m. They agreed.

In 1916, following the Easter Rising, the homes of known Sinn Féin supporters and other 'suspects' were raided on Saturday 6 May. Among those arrested was Richard

Corish. St Brigid's Home for Inebriates, the Royal Irish Constabulary Barracks at 69 South Main Street, and the Military Barracks at Barrack Street were used as prisons until the detainees could be sent to Dublin.

In June 1920, 400 extra troops arrived via Rosslare Harbour, their destination being Wexford Military Barracks. In September 1920, forty members of the Devonshire Regiment, stationed at the Barracks, ran amok on Wexford's streets. They accosted civilians with demands to know where the Sinn Féin Club was, and not satisfied with the replies, they assaulted the people questioned. The RIC tried to intervene but their requests for assistance to troops at the Barracks went unheeded. Finally the local people could take no more and hit back. Fights broke out on the Main Street and at the Bullring, with stones and bottles thrown. Eventually the soldiers were driven back to the headquarters.

The inauguration of the Irish Republic was marked in Wexford in 1949 with a huge procession through the town. The FCA, the Old IRA, and members of political parties and social clubs marched with other uniformed bodies and the town's bands from the Military Barracks via Main Street, Rowe Street, and School Street to St Peter's Square. There the tricolour flew at half mast. Brendan Corish TD read the 1916 Proclamation and the flag was raised. Three volleys were fired by the FCA. The bands played 'Faith of Our Fathers' and the national anthem, and then led the parade back to Barrack Street.

Batt Street towards the Cott Safe. Note the roofs of the houses and the very practical ramps leading to the doors. These would have been ideal for prams. (*Dominic Kiernan Collection.*)

Batt Street

Origins and Meaning

Batt Street takes its name from the owner of the land, Jane Batt. The family name is associated with the Cromwellian settlement.

It was also known as Byrnes Lane. Byrnes lived at 1 Batt Street.

Earliest Mentions

Batt Street is listed in Griffith's Valuation.

Buildings

Slaney Minerals had a bottling plant in Batt Street.

A chip shop named Keane's and Doran's, who made statues, were both located there. There were also a number of stables, and in one of them some locals put on plays including *Murder in the Red Barn*, where the smell of donkey droppings surely added authenticity to the production.

Batt Street from the Cott Safe end. (*Dominic Kiernan Collection.*)

Hogan, the blacksmith, opened his business in 1939.

Lett's fish and shellfish factory opened in June 1969.

In Griffith's Valuation Jane Batt, who also had large holdings throughout the town, owns the major portion of the street. Other landowners in Batt Street included: Martin Byrne; James Keating; Nicholas Murphy; Dennis Sinnott; Francis Furlong; Elizabeth Cullen; James Keating, and Christopher Codd.

People and Events

An advertisement in 1902 quoted John Ruth of Batt Street, a fisherman using Dean's Backache Kidney Pills at 2s 9d a box.

Also in 1902 Bartholomew Carty, Batt Street, was summoned for children's non-attendance at school. His wife stated that he was often at sea and she was unwell and unable to ensure schooling. He was fined 1s and 1s 6d costs. Eleven similar cases were fined on the same day.

Michael Fenlon of Batt Street was fined 1s in 1902 for obstructing the street by dumping a cartload of apples.

In 1912 there was an air show in Wexford Park and a plane actually took off from there, only to lose power and crash at the Cott Safe off Batt Street.

In 1914 Ellen Murphy of William Street applied to have three boys named Kavanagh committed to the industrial school. Inspector Sullivan, NSPCC, said they lived with their mother in a small wooden hut on the strand below Batt Street. Head Constable McGrath said the father was a sort of 'fresh-water pirate'.

In 1917 an application from J. Lett of Batt Street for permission to use the foreshore near Star Engineering to dry his nets was rejected by the corporation. It was pointed out that the space is free to all, no rent is paid for it, and therefore there can be no exclusive right.

Woolworth's announced that the opening of their Wexford store would take place at 9a.m. on Friday 4 April 1952. Suppliers advertising their involvement included, 'All smith work and iron plating was carried out by M. Hogan & Son of Batt Street.'

Other

Access to the Cott Safe and Browne's Bank was restricted to those owning boats, and a watchman was in place to uphold the regulations.

Boker (The)

Origins and Meaning
The Boker is generally thought to be a corruption taken from Gaelic for road 'bothar'.

The Boker was the colloquial name for the nearby CBS School.

It is also known as Joseph Street in honour of St Joseph.

Earliest Mentions
The corporation built the street in the 1870s on land given by James Roche, PP.

It was named Joseph Street in 1877 after the school of that name operated by the Christian Brothers.

Neither Joseph Street nor the Boker are listed in Griffith's Valuation.

Buildings
Richard Devereux provided the Christian Brothers with a monastery at the Boker, where they still reside. Among the subjects taught by them were Navigation and Astronomy. The foundation stone of the monastery at Joseph Street was laid on 31 March 1873.

Other
At the rear of the Christian Brothers' house in the Boker is a flat area and a steep hill leading to the Secondary College. It is said that it was here that the hill was dug out to provide ballast for Wexford port.

Bride Street

Origins and Meaning
Bride Street takes its name from the parish of St Bridget.

One of the original gates of the walled town was Bride's Gate.

Earliest Mentions
The name Bride Street was used in 1650.

In 1659 it is classed as a suburb and is called 'Bridestrette'. The population of the street is given as thirteen Irish and two English.

'A yard to the street, and a cabin or shed in it, in St Bride Street, Wexford', is documented in 1680.

Dr Hadden, in his work on Wexford, speculated that, 'From the fisheries around the Bishopswater and Oyster Lane area ran two corresponding link routes; one up Bride Street to join the Market trail at the ford of Slippery Green.'

Buildings

Bride Street Churchyard was also called St Bridget's. The ruins of St Bridget's were noted at Bride's Gate in 1800. The corner of the current yard was a Quaker graveyard. The altar stone outside the church is from St James's, Kerlogue, which was founded by Military Order of Knights Templar. The altar stone was used in Penal times and brought to town in 1887. It was moved to the present site in 1956, when the stones were numbered and re-assembled.

The cross was erected to commemorate a Redemptorist mission in 1858. The cross was replaced in 2008. The cobblestones at the door are from Rosslare Fort and are called a Wexford Mosaic.

The Adoration Convent is in the grounds of Bride Street church. Bishop Furlong

Bride Street, with two modes of transport that lived side by side fifty years ago. There appear to be two shops opposite each other here, according to the cigarette advertising signs. (*Dominic Kiernan Collection.*)

founded the original convent at Rockfield in 1870. The nuns moved to Bride Street on 1 May 1887. Besides a life devoted to prayer, the Sisters make altar bread and vestments and are always ready to listen to the problems of the townspeople.

In a list of corporation leases we find, 'By indenture executed to Catherine Redmond in 1774 she became seized of a piece of ground adjoining the Town Wall and Bride Street at the yearly rent of 5s 5d for the term of thirty-one years.'

Some of the houses, such as No.9 Bride Street, date to the 1860s and may incorporate earlier buildings.

Seven houses at Bride Street and Clifford Street were let in 1887 at 2s 3d and 2s per week.

Griffith's Valuation shows landowners in Bride Street as: Villiers Hatton; John Furlong; William Lee; Robert Anglin; Hamilton Morgan; William Radford; Richard Ryan; Nicholas Whitty; Mary Kelly; John E. Redmond; John Barden; James Talbot; Edward Dixon; Patrick Jordan; Mary Murphy; James Clifford; Hannah Elms; Francis Harpur; William Trigg, and John McParland.

There is also mention of the Roman Catholic church in progress on land owned by St Bridget's Chapel Committee.

People and Events

John Barry of Wexford laboured as a secular priest for many years in Augusta, Georgia, and was consecrated second Bishop of Savannah, on 2 August 1857. He ruled but two years, and was present at the dedication of Bride Street church, Wexford, on 11 September 1859. His death occurred two months later on 21 November.

Michael Hayes was born c.1867, the son of another Michael Hayes. He lived in Bride Street and Bride Place. He was a sailor in 1897 when his first child was born and a labourer in 1902 when his second child was born. His wife Ellen died in 1910 in Gibson Street.

In 1884 tontine societies were asked by the Mayor to only advertise locally. St Joseph's Tontine Mortality, at No. 3 Bride Place, met to discuss the advertisement. John McCabe was in the chair. Thomas Doyle (carpenter), Richard Keeffe (gas fitter) and John Connas (saddler) resolved on behalf of Wexford Trade Societies to request its removal.

In May 1889 the Relieving Officer, Mr Murphy, presented a request to the Board of Guardians from a woman named Connors living at Bride Street, that her outdoor relief payment be increased as her children were starving. After discussion it was raised by 6d to 2s 6d.

In 1902 Ellen Sheridan, Bride Street, summoned Alice Connors for indecent and provoking language, stating that Connors said, 'Are you able to puck me you old cockle raking duffer.' Connors counter claimed. Sgt Fennell said both were as bad as each other. Connors was fined £2 or one month, and Sheridan 10s 6d or fourteen days.

Some boys were fined 2s 6d for playing handball at Bride Street in 1903.

During the Lockout in 1911, a baton charge at Bride Street resulted in John Carroll, a resident of the street, receiving 'nasty scalp wounds'.

At the Petty Sessions in 1914, Peter Cleary of Roche's Terrace was fined 1s for allowing his goat to wander in Bride Street.

In the same year this sad report appeared in the newspaper:

> John Radford of Furlongs Lane, Bride Street, a quay porter, was found at his home, where he lived with his mother. He was lying on the kitchen floor with a gash in his throat. A bloodstained razor was under his head. Constables were called. One cycled for Dr Pierse who pronounced the man extinct. He had been in the asylum and had made previous suicide attempts. In a letter found, he stated, 'John Radford, born 7 March 1881. Pray for the soul of John Radford who died 14 April 1914.' The date was crossed out and 1 July inserted, indicating his earlier intention.

With the end of the First World War, flags, bunting and blazing tar barrels appeared on Wexford's streets. An impromptu parade led by St Brigid's Fife and Drum Band (referred to in reports as the Bride Street Band) marched through the town. The parade paused outside John Street graveyard and cheers were raised for the Redmond family who were buried there, in recognition of their contribution to Wexford.

An indication of work practices on the quays was illustrated on 11 November 1931. John Butler of Bride Street and Matthew Stafford of Ram Street applied for the position of Weigh Master in charge of the weighbridge at Crescent Quay. Mr Butler, a disabled ex-serviceman on a pension of 12s per week offered 2s per week to hire the weighbridge. Mr Stafford offered 5s per week. Stafford was appointed.

The position of Harbour Master was also vacant that year following the resignation of Captain J. Saunders. The following people applied for the job: Charles Kehoe, harbour constable, Bride Street; James Carroll, the Faythe; Michael Doyle, Barrack Street; Patrick Hawkins, Michael Street; Captain D. Murphy, temporary pilot, Clifford Street; Captain Thomas Morris, pilot master, Carrigeen Street; William Bent, Bride Place, and Edward Wickham, North Main Street.

Three people were hospitalised following a fire at Nellie Wright's Bride Street chip shop in July 1970.

Other

The Bride Street/Main Street corner was called Coffin Corner in 1812.

During excavation for the building now standing to the north of the Bride Street/Main Street junction, evidence of our Viking past was uncovered.

In 1968, Hackney Cars had these rates: Bride Street – Crosstown, £1 10s 0d; Rowe Street – Crosstown, £1 5s 0d; Ninth day, 15s; weddings, £1 10s 0d; christening, 12s 6d.

In Coolcotts Lane lived one of the characters of the 1940s, Sam Wetherald. His family had owned property at the back of Bride Street towards the Stonebridge called Wetherald's Court. He had a monkey and a sailor's cap and a liking for porter. When he made his way home in the evenings, and was in danger of colliding with the wall, the local boys would call out, 'Port your helm Sam, port your helm.'

The Bullring

Origins and Meaning

The familiar name Bullring is derived from a sport introduced in 1621. In that year the butchers' guild received their charter, part of which required them to provide a bull for baiting on 24 August and on 21 November of each year, the hides of which would be presented to the Mayor. The sport of bull-baiting consisted of a beast being fastened by its horns to a stake in the ground via a 15ft length of rope. The spectators then formed a circle holding their dogs ready. One dog was released and tried to get beneath the bull to attack the stomach. The bull often managed to toss the dog as high as 30ft in the air, but in the end the larger beast always lost. He was savagely bitten by the dogs to the delight of the crowd, and eventually died. Bull-baiting continued in the Bullring until about 1770. It then moved to a yard near John Street and Parliamentary candidates provided the bulls, with the carcasses going to feed the poor of the town.

Earliest Mentions

Before 1621, the area of the Bullring was called 'The Common Plain' and this may indicate the origin of the Common Quay, probably an area of free access to the waterfront. In 1790 the Bullring became known as Fountain Square when the Marquis of Ely erected a fountain there. The fountain was removed to Cornmarket in 1800 and the name of the Bullring has remained since.

In 1833 it was stated to be unlit and unpaved.

Buildings

Opposite the New Market at Common Quay Street were Kavanagh's premises. This was the first garage in Wexford. It opened on 14 December 1914, selling 'Pratt's Perfection Spirit' petrol in two-gallon cans at 2s 4d each. The system then was to carry these cans on the running board of the car until the engine ran low

The Gut, when Sloan's dominated that corner. (*Dominic Kiernan Collection.*)

on fuel. The first Wexford petrol pump was erected here in 1919. A fire-engine house was located here, as noted on a map of 1880.

The original Courthouse spanned Main Street, facing Cape, with a lane accessing The Gut. There appears to have been some opposition to the demolition of the old Court House, for at the Assizes it was ordered that the materials of the Court House be sold to the highest bidder within fourteen days.

The Corporation, who had until then held their meetings in the Court House, were barred from the new Court House on the Quay. To provide new premises, they purchased 60ft of the former Shambles from Mr Sparrow. There they built the Tholsel, with the Council Chamber and offices above and the Fish Market on the ground floor, entered by way of five arches. The National Irish Bank, formerly the Northern Bank, once Traynor's seed merchants and hardware stores, is built on the site of the Tholsel. The Court of Conscience for debts under 40s and corporation offices were at the Tholsel in 1837, with the butter market underneath. The Tholsel was demolished in 1898.

In the corner of the Bullring beside the meat market is a boutique. This shop is on the site of a building that has been Lambert's Pub, Morris's Hotel, Pitts's Coaching Inn, and the rectory of Archdeacon Elgee, who was a grandfather of 'Speranza', Lady Wilde, mother of Oscar.

The Bullring, possibly dating from the 1940s. The vehicles here are military. (*Dominic Kiernan Collection*.)

The Bullring fountain that once saw the area called Fountain Square. (*Dominic Kiernan Collection*.)

Macken's 'Cape' bar was called the 'Cape of Good Hope', another reminder of Wexford's nautical past. Lord Kingsborough was held here in 1798. This establishment was the home of the 'Thirteen Club', where members were required to consume thirteen glasses of punch in quick succession! A 'Cape Club' was formed in September 1834, composed of government officials and upper-class shopkeepers.

The stone-walled building in the Bullring is called the New Market. This was built in 1871; the north-side buildings replaced six thatched houses as a marketplace for traders coming from the country, in an attempt to regularise the marketing. Prior to that meat was sold in the Shambles or meat market, which was located at various places in the town (Anne Street, Archer's Lane, etc.). Butter was sold at the Tholsel and fish in the Bullring. Corn and potatoes were sold at Cornmarket and poultry on the public streets. The hope was that all would now be sold in one marketplace. On 6 May 1872 it was noted that the Corporation had been allowed to borrow £1,000 to erect the new market. Tolls at the New Market included fowl at 1*d* per basket and turkeys at 1*d* each at Christmas.

In 1881, Laurence Murphy sold stationery next to Daly's Bakery. Fortune & Murphy were selling New Masses and Offices to clergy at that time.

The fire engine station was at John's Gate Street and the hose station was at the New Market in the Bullring in 1910.

'Radio-Vision', Wexford's first television store, was opened at the Bullring in July 1952.

People and Events

Between the years 1770 and 1780, the Redmond's Bank was founded by Walter and Thomas Redmond and it was flourishing in 1785. Redmond's Bank was in the Bullring in a house later occupied by James Kelly, grocer. In 1811 it was robbed by Archibald and Isaac Wood, who lived next door. They are said to have hidden the proceeds in a large kettle that acted as a sign over their shop. They were later uncovered and Archibald was sentenced to be burned on the hand and transported for seven years. Isaac was acquitted. When the bank failed in 1834 all creditors were paid and business was transferred to the new local branch of Bank of Ireland with John E. Redmond as manager.

There is little concrete evidence that a Cromwellian Massacre occurred in the Bullring. In 1798 an open-air forge operated there for pike manufacture, perhaps making good use of Ely's Fountain.

On 2 June 1798, the patrol boats captured a ship in the outer harbour. On board were three officers, including Lord Kingsborough. They had been in Dublin when the rebellion started and hurried back to Wexford thinking that so secure a town would not fall so easily. Lord Kingsborough was lodged at Captain Keogh's house until the people demanded that he be imprisoned. The gaol was full, and therefore

Kingsborough was put under guard at a house in the Bullring (now The Cape Bar), near the main guardhouse.

That insurrection of 1798 is commemorated by Oliver Sheppard's statue of a Pikeman. It was unveiled on Sunday 6 August 1905 by Fr Kavanagh, OFM, a popular historian of the period. Eleven special trains carried spectators to Wexford for the ceremony and a parade of more than twenty bands passed through almost every street in the town. Sheppard was the sculptor responsible for many of Co. Wexford's '98 memorials and it was he who executed the Cúchullain Statue in Dublin's GPO.

At the Quarter Sessions in January 1831, Pat Doyle received a sentence of six months confinement for assault. Miles Dillon was sentenced to nine months, including the treadmill, for stealing forty-three sheaves of barley. John Byrne was to be whipped privately and kept in solitary confinement for two calendar months for stealing ropes, according to *The Wexford Independent*.

Hannah Murphy, a woman of easy virtue, was charged with stealing a silk handkerchief, property of Margaret Byrne. Byrne stated that she met the defendant at the piazza (probably the Bullring) where she took the item. The next morning she identified the handkerchief in Mr Tennant's pawnshop. No verdict was recorded in the newspaper but His Worship stated, 'If she was charged with public robbery she would be hanged.' The attention of the constabulary was also called to the number of bull and mastiff dogs prowling streets, especially in John Street and Hill Street.

In 1831 Ambrose Fortune manufactured razors, penknives, etc., to the highest standard in premises near the Bullring. There was also a clock and watch business.

Mr Thomas Jefferies lived in Mr P. Hynes's drapery shop in the Bullring in 1840.

In 1870 the press reported a 'unanimous resolution in favour of establishing a monthly fair, to be held between the Bullring and down along the quays'. All other fairs were to be suppressed.

In 1881 Fortune & Murphy of Bullring (opposite New Market) were selling stereoscope slides, birthday cards, and whitewood souvenirs of Wexford, with views of remarkable places in the county.

The Bullring has long been the venue of rallies and protests, and has echoed to the voices of almost every politician of note during the past few centuries. James Larkin, Éamon De Valera, John Redmond and Peter Daly were among those who addressed Wexfordmen in this historic spot. A Suffragette Meeting was held there in April 1914, and a Recruitment Rally in June 1915. An Anti-Vaccination Protest attracted a large crowd in 1919. Throughout the years, celebrations for numerous sporting wins have centred on the Bullring.

There is a plaque on the wall of the bank, to honour one of Wexford's sporting heroes, Jem Roche. Roche is probably best known for his unsuccessful challenge for the World Heavyweight Boxing Championship against T. Burns in Dublin on St Patrick's Day, 1908. In a career of thirty-eight fights, he won twenty-two by knockout and seven on points. One of those he knocked out was John L. Sullivan. Roche's many friends and admirers erected the plaque in 1961.

Other

The Bullring itself was originally a beach on the seafront, which probably curved from St Iberius church to the Rock of Wexford.

A clue to the location of the medieval shoreline was provided in March 1991. A trench dug in the Bullring exposed sea sand about three meters below the present road surface. An oak pile (or timber) was embedded in the sand.

Carrigeen Street

Origins and Meaning

The literal translation of Carrigeen is 'little rock'. The topography of the street still reflects this name, as it is built on a rocky outcrop.

Earliest Mentions

Although not mentioned by name in the actual chronicles, Carrigeen played a pivotal part in the history of Wexford during 1169. The Norman army approached the town, crossed the Bishopswater River and reached the high ground where Carrigeen is situated today. There, the Norman leader Robert Fitzstephen deployed his archers, with a commanding view of the town's defences.

John O'Donovan recorded information about the holy wells located in Wexford Town in 1840. All of these have since vanished. St Peter's well was located in the townland of Carrick, at the Carrigeen Street–Old Pound junction approximately, and in 1840 its water was used for domestic purposes.

Buildings

The Kilmaine Estate offered houses at Carrigeen on weekly tenancy terminable every Monday. The tenants included:

No. 1, Ellen Walsh, house and garden, 1s.

No. 2, Bridget Murphy, house, yard and garden.

No. 4, Edward Murphy, house and yard, 9d.

No.-, Nicholas Cullen, house and yard, 10d.

No. 6 and No. 6a, Robert Jordan, house, yard and garden.

No. 26, R. Walsh, house, yard and garden.

Carrigeen is notable as it was here, and in Roche's Terrace, that the first artisan dwellings were constructed by Wexford Corporation. On 17 November 1887 Wexford Corporation purchased a parcel of land at Carrigeen/Roche's Road for £150. They borrowed £2,500 and decided to build houses based on the design of those at Trinity Street. Philip Lacey of Wexford won the tender to build six at £77 per house and another four at £76 10s 0d each. Aidan Redmond of Georges Street won a tender to build another three at £89 15s 0d each. The building was completed in 1889 and tenants paid 2s 4d a week in rent.

A land auction in 1920 included the following properties of Lady Maurice Fitzgerald: Labour Exchange; most of Carrigeen; Market House and Town Hall; Cinema Palace; Heffernans; Belvedere, and Johns Hill.

In Griffith's Valuation the primary landowners were: Mathew Talbot; Charles Harvey; Patrick Jordan; John Guilfoyle; Mary Talbot; Richard Walsh; John Cullen, and Sir William Geary. The Fever Hospital was included in the street.

People and Events
In the newspapers of 1823 there were reports that a child, in absence of its nurse, fell into fire in a house in Carrigeen. The child later died.

Among the casualties of the Ardcavan boating tragedy of 1900 was William Duggan of Carrigeen Street, who was the Bishop's coachman. William Duggan left a wife and six children.

In September 1902 George Whitmore of Carrigeen fell from a pile at Commercial Quay at 7.45p.m. on Tuesday. The splash was heard by two Enniscorthy cottmen who tried to rescue him with a pole. They looked for someone to jump in but it was a while before John Rossiter of Crosstown did so, and he pulled the exhausted man from the full tide. Unfortunately Whitmore died some hours later.

The CYMS held a carnival in Kirwan's field in 1951, and Mc Fadden's Roadshow performed there in 1953. These were regular entertainments in the middle of the twentieth century. Kirwan's was also called 'The Circus Field'. Our Lady of Fatima School is on the site of Kirwan's Field.

Castle Hill Street

Origins and Meaning
The older name of Castle Hill Street is said to come from Wexford Castle (later replaced by the military barracks of Barrack Street). The hill above the castle leading to the Faythe was referred to as Castle Hills around 1840. Another tradition referred to Taylor's Castle, a house and estate that stood between this hill and

Castle Hill Street may take its name from this building. It is Taylor's Castle.

the seafront but this would give a much later naming. Taylor's Castle was built in around 1775 and was in use in 1840. It was still standing in 1903 but mostly demolished between then and 1941.

The current official name refers to the Irish patriot Kevin Barry, made famous in a song of the same name. The name was originally changed in September 1920. In 1932 a plebiscite was taken to legalise this decision.

Earliest Mentions

The street is extant but not named in early maps.

The houses are depicted in a map of 1831, before the opening of Parnell Street.

Buildings

James Furlong purchased five houses in Castle Hill Street for £500.

In Griffith's Valuation the street is simply called Castle Hill. Of fifteen houses noted, most are on land owned by Patience Tottenham or the reps of John Hughes. James Carr owned the remaining plot.

People and Events

The records for 1864 show thirty-seven shipmasters in Wexford, among them John

Castle Hill Street from the Faythe, with St Michael's Graveyard behind the white wall. The pending procession has an altar on the entrance steps. (*Dominic Kiernan Collection*.)

Hore of Castle Street (referring to either Castle Hill Street or Barrack Street).

Other

A church dedicated to St Michael was located at the top of Castle Hill Street. This incorporated the Norse burial ground outside the walls.

Charlotte Street

Origins and Meaning

It is probably named for Charlotte, Princess of Wales, who died in 1817.

It was officially renamed Colbert Street on 1 September 1920. In 1932, a plebiscite was taken to legalise this decision but it was not passed and the change could not be legalised. A further decision was made in 1981 to make the alteration.

Earliest Mentions

Charlotte Street was originally known as Custom House Lane.

In 1828 there was a request that the 'street be powder paved – new street at custom house'.

The name changed in the early 1800s, as evidenced by a Harbour Commissioner note of 1830, 'Widened street at Old Custom House now called Charlotte Street.'

Gaffney's Lane was an old title of Charlotte Street, after the Gaffneys, ship owners.

Buildings

The Centenary Stores was mentioned in Charlotte Street in 1902 but probably dates from around 1850.

A decree was obtained at Petty Sessions by Miss K. Pitt, North Main Street, for possession of house held by William Hall at Courthouse Lane (probably Charlotte Street) in September 1914.

Kinsella's coal yard had a side entrance from Charlotte Street, with scales for weighing pigs. This is now the exit from the car park.

On the south-east corner of Charlotte Street was Doyle's Plumbers. This was possibly the nineteenth-century post office.

In Griffith's Valuation the landowners include: Frances Murphy; Robert Hughes; Catherine Kehoe; James Browne; Philip Murphy; Denis Kehoe, and William Walker.

People and Events

In the 1800s Charlotte Street was home to the coach terminal, 'Shamrock Coach Co. leaves Thomas Kehoe's, Charlotte Street at 6.00 a.m.; arrives College Green, Dublin (White Horse Cellar) at 6.00 p.m. Fare 8s.'

According to the diary of Edward Solly Flood, a floating cholera hospital was built in Wexford in 1893 by James Doyle & Co. of Charlotte Street to designs by E.K. Ryan (CE JP), ready to be moored in the Coal Channel under the yellow quarantine flag.

Doyle's were plumbers based at Charlotte Street in 1893.

In 1917 Walter Carter of Charlotte Street was fined 6d for playing football on the street. He said that on returning from the chapel some children had kicked the ball to him and he kicked it back. The constable stated that Carter had picked up the ball (a football case filled with hay) and kicked it from Charlotte Street into Main Street. This caused inconvenience to people using the street for business or pleasure.

In November of the same year there was a letter from the Town Clerk, with a report from the Medical Officer of Health, relating to the sanitary conditions of a lane adjacent to Charlotte Street. A committee was appointed to inspect the lane.

Other

We sometimes forget the association that Charlotte Street had with labour relations and unions in the past. The first trade union movement was founded in Wexford in 1843. Previously there had been several trade societies established for particular handicrafts, but that year the need to have all the artisans of the town welded together on the old principle of unity in action became clearly recognised.

In 1843 a representative meeting was held in a house then occupied by Thomas Daly on the corner of Charlotte Street. The promoters of this gathering were: Messrs Nicholas Campbell, rope-maker, the Faythe; Tom Hynes, hatter, John Street; James Clancy, painter, Old Pound; Nicholas Brien, baker, John Street; George Codd, shoemaker, George Street; Henry Donohoe, shoemaker, and Ben Hughes of the *Wexford Independent*.

This may have been the same building to feature in 1912, when, on the afternoon of Saturday 27 January, T.P. Daly was arrested as he sat in the Transport Union office in Charlotte Street. At first it was thought that he was being arrested for non-payment of a £10 fine imposed for 'persistently following' the blacklegs working at Pierce's. In fact Daly was charged with 'incitement' further to remarks he had made at a public meeting.

In February of that year seven fitters from Leeds arrived in Wexford and proceeded to Pierce's, where they were to receive 34s to 38s a week for fitting agricultural machinery and bicycles. They became suspicious when they saw the heavy police presence in Wexford and their first knowledge of a lockout was when they saw it mentioned on a newspaper placard outside a shop. By 1p.m. they had left the foundry and gone to the Transport Union office in Charlotte Street, where they gave full details of how they had been misled. That same evening they were guests on the platform at a huge rally addressed by James Connolly, who had arrived in Wexford. One of the Leeds fitters, named Simpson, was 'enthusiastically received' by the crowd and, on behalf of his colleagues he declared full solidarity with the struggle in Wexford. The Leeds fitters departed the following morning.

Clifford Street

Origins and Meaning
Clifford Street was built on land owned by Clifford's of Ashfield. Major Clifford of Ashfield lived at one time in Cromwell's Fort.

Earliest Mentions
It is not in the map of 1649 or that of the early 1800s.
Clifford Street is listed in Griffith's Valuation.

Buildings
Seven houses at Bride Street and Clifford Street were let at 2s 3d and 2s per week in 1887.

Clifford Street taken from Bride Street. (*Dominic Kiernan Collection.*)

A number of the houses here date to the 1880s.

In Griffith's Valuation James Naster, Villiers Hatton and William Gibson are listed as landowners, along with John E. Redmond and James Clifford.

People and Events

In October 1902 Wexford Corporation employed twenty-four men to lay a footpath at Clifford Street.

In 1914 L. Furlong, who lived at 2 Clifford Terrace, was the agent for Bandon Distillery.

James Gaul of Clifford Street captained *Kerlogue* in 1942.

Common Quay Street

Origins and Meaning

Common Quay Street is believed to take its name from the Common Quay. This in turn may owe its origins to a concept similar to 'the commons' in land terms,

Common Quay Street, facing towards the Bullring. (*Dominic Kiernan Collection.*)

Common Quay
Street in the
twentieth century.
The Slaney Bar
and the store have
been replaced
by the Bank of
Ireland building.
(*Dominic Kiernan
Collection.*)

which would denote a quay where those without a private quay or wharf could land goods prior to the quay improvements of the early 1800s.

In his article in the *Wexford Historical Society Journal* on medieval Wexford, Billy Colfer states, 'The area just outside the Norse town – the present Bullring – seems to have been held in common by both 'sides'. In 1621 it was referred to as the Common Plain, and the quay there was known as Common Quay, a name still surviving in Common Quay Street.'

The official name was changed to O'Hanlon Walsh Street in 1920. In 1932 a plebiscite was taken to legalise this decision but it was not passed and the change could not be legalised. A further decision was made in 1981 to make the alteration.

Earliest Mentions

On the maps of earlier times the street is noted as Common Quay, as it offered water access on the south side before the quay improvements.

Buildings

Fred Woods's Printing Works may have been a remodelled Salt Store, or built on the site of a Salt Store. It was later intended for use as a working men's Temperance Coffee House, established by the St Iberius Church of Ireland Society for mariners or tradesmen based at the nearby quays.

In 1856 the CYMS was established here. The building is dated 1877. This club was a popular venue for many types of entertainment and some people recall entering the doors at today's Halifax Bank office to attend dances, drama performances and even cage bird shows. At the rear of the premises the CYMS Billiard/Snooker Hall was located. It may originally have been the Muskerry town house.

Common Quay Street was the location of Harry Wilson's coal importers head office and depot.

Next door the modernised building is Iberius House.

In Griffith's Valuation, Common Quay Street shows lands owned by: James Roche; Denis Doyle; William Bell and Eliza Wheeler; Patrick Sinnott; John E. Redmond; Hamilton Morgan; Anne Redmond, and Nathaniel Sparrow. The mayor's office and market house were also noted.

People and Events

A man named Glascott from the parish of Tintern shot himself in Common Quay Lane in 1861. He was at once conveyed to the County Infirmary, where every attention was paid him, but died shortly after admission.

The best-known eating houses were said to be in Common Quay Lane –

Cluney's, Somer's and Mrs Doyle's. Steak and onions was the most popular dish. One of these Common Quay Street refreshment rooms was advertised by New Market in 1879. A cup of tea, hot and fresh cost 1*d*; a cup of coffee in perfection, 1*d*; chops and steaks, 6*d*. Lenten dishes were specially prepared for Friday and fast days in Lent. A bowl of meat soup cost 2*d*. They offered a parcel office free to customers.

Cornmarket

Origins and Meaning

This area was on the periphery of the old Celtic settlement around Selskar before the Vikings ever crossed the bar of the harbour. With the Norman arrival and occupation, it got its name and designation as the only legitimate part of Wexford for the sale of corn that was brought to town by the farmers of the countryside.

Earliest Mentions

Cornmarket was listed in 1764.

In 1808, three 'lately built houses near the Cornmarket' belonging to Mrs Harvey were to let with all applications to go to N. Vicary. 'The Houses are laid out with shops and are well situated for business.'

There was a corn and potato market here in 1837 and the fountain from the Bullring was located here between 1800 and 1890.

Dr Hadden, with a keen eye for land and seascape and unrivalled knowledge of the history of Wexford town, postulated the existence of a prehistoric market located around the present Cornmarket, centuries before the arrival of the Vikings, according to Edward Culleton in the *Wexford Historical Society Journal* in an article on Norse Wexford.

Buildings

Five premises were on the site where Patrick Kelly's now stands. One of the most interesting was the Bethesda church. This later became a theatre.

Cornmarket had at least twenty shops in the 1880s including 'The Shelburne Hotel' or 'Flying Flea', which catered for men of the road.

In an article on Bishop Sweetman in the *Wexford Historical Society Journal*, Nicholas Furlong states that in the 1700s, 'Cornmarket and the streets adjoining were the shopping centre of the town.'

The Arts Centre dates back to the 1700s when it was built as The Assembly

Cornmarket, with a wonderful view of Carroll's shop that shows how goods were displayed in the early twentieth century. (*Dominic Kiernan Collection.*)

Cornmarket towards Main Street. Note the array of businesses on the left. (*Dominic Kiernan Collection.*)

Cornmarket, with the Town Hall (now the Arts Centre) dominating the scene. Note the narrow house to its right. (*Dominic Kiernan Collection.*)

Cornmarket opened onto Main Street through the Gut, shown here with the dog giving some perspective. The posters for *Airport* at the Abbey and 'Star Trek Disco' at White's, together with band names like 'The Teenbeats' and 'The Real McCoy' date this to the early 1970s. (*Dominic Kiernan Collection.*)

Rooms, with a ballroom and market area combined. In 1772 the corporation purchased a piece of land 'fronted by Cornmarket' from John Grogan of Johnstown Castle. Mr Hatchell undertook the contract to build the market house and he completed the task by 1776. The cost was £1,240 5s. It was built to an L-shaped plan with a series of five round-headed openings to the ground floor originally forming an open arcade, and two bay two-storey returns to the west. After 1849 it was in use as a ballroom. It also functioned as a lecture space, where hundreds of workers heard of the wonders of science, and performers like Percy French appeared regularly. It reverted to the arts in 1974 and continues to thrive as a wonderful venue.

'The Ark', now Thomas Moore Tavern, dates from around 1750 and was originally a favourite haunt of 'nocturnal oyster eaters', who would pay 10d for one hundred. The Ark Club was popular with keepers of small shops and well-to-do tradesmen in 1834. Thomas Moore, on being honoured by the Slaney Amateur Society, referred to his grandfather as 'honest Tom Codd of Cornmarket'. It was later Molly Mythen's.

In Griffith's Valuation the landowners of Cornmarket were: Mary Byrne; Richard Fitzgerald; John Cullen; Laurence Roche; Villiers Hatton; John Richards; Mary Murphy; Sarah Hamilton; Henry Mullen; Rudford Daniel; Thomas Jeffries; Hamilton Morgan, and the executors of James Colfer.

People and Events

The Corporation (now Wexford Borough Council) met at the Town Hall in Cornmarket before they moved to the Municipal Buildings on 5 February 1951. The building was more accessible to the public as a dance hall where such luminaries as Johnny Reck, Elvis Murphy and Larry Kirwan brought the sounds of the pop world to Wexford.

Constable Power summoned Thomas Kelly of Cornmarket for being drunk and assaulting Michael Redmond. The defendant said, 'when he got a sup he went mad but he had now taken the pledge'.

Nicholas Kinsella was charged with 'furious driving of a horse and cart laden with fowl at Cornmarket, causing people to flee for their lives on a public street'. He was fined 10s and costs.

Back in 1807 Mrs Bridget Kehoe, linen draper, Cornmarket, was seized with an apoplectic fit while serving a customer and died two days later.

In 1809, a meadow of 3½ acres lately owned by Pat Furlong of Cornmarket was to let, situated half a mile from town.

The Brunswick Club was formed in 1828 at the Assembly Rooms (the present-day Arts Centre), in Cornmarket. The Brunswick was explicitly Protestant and Loyalist and preached against the Nationalist cause.

Cornmarket in the late 1970s. (*Dominic Kiernan Collection.*)

Cornmarket. Cobbler Paddy Healy at work in his shop in the mid-twentieth century. (*Dominic Kiernan Collection.*)

In 1824, Sheffield & Co. painters, glaziers and paper stainers operated in Cornmarket.

The Earl of Mulgrave, Viceroy of Ireland, visited Wexford in 1836. He arrived at the Courthouse on the quay accompanied by a company of Hussars. A number of cannon from a private collection of Grogan-Morgan of Johnstown Castle fired a salute on the quay. The Viceroy then paraded along the waterfront, past the gasworks, up New Road (now Parnell Street) to the Faythe and back along Main Street. After tea at Bettyville, he attended a banquet at the Assembly Rooms, Cornmarket.

In 1902 Anastasia Doyle, Cornmarket, was accused of throwing water at the window of Mrs Connor's shops, damaging goods, tea, sugar and bread. Witnesses said she was only washing her own windows.

John Smith, a billposter from Cornmarket, was summoned in 1902 for assault on Anastasia Whelan. She said that on 26 July he threw two stones at her. The Head Constable said that the boy was a constant cause of complaint. A place in a reformatory was to be sought for him. Meanwhile, both left by separate doors. Outside he threatened Whelan again; she reported this to the police and an arrest warrant was issued.

In the same year, Mary Whelan of John Street, summoned Mary Doyle of Cornmarket for abusive and threatening language. She stated that Doyle called her bad names after previous petty sessions and added 'that she would be dead before the rising of the moon for herself and her father would be on their knees praying for her sudden death'.

Wexford's first corps of Volunteers was formed in 1914. This national force had been growing rapidly for months, rallying to 'the Cause of Irish Independence'. The Wexford corps grew from a meeting at the Assembly Rooms in Cornmarket.

In 1917 Private A. O'Brien from Cornmarket, serving with the 6th Royal Irish Regiment, received a commendation. His brother fell at Mons.

There was an air-raid shelter here in 1941.

You could have your boots soled and heeled by Paddy Healey in Cornmarket in the mid-twentieth century.

Other

Beside the Thomas Moore there was an old entrance to White's Barn, the dance Mecca of Wexford in the mid-1900s. Remember the sheepskin jackets, the 'bum freezers', the fights and the smell of spilt Guinness?

Michael Hayes was born to Michael Hayes and his wife Margaret McDonald in 1867. They lived in Cornmarket and the father's occupation was shopkeeper.

Davitt Road

Origins and Meaning

Davitt Road is named in honour of Michael Davitt, who addressed a Wexford meeting on 21 October 1883.

The present area of Davitt Road amalgamates the older development of Davitt Road North and South with newer developments at Davitt Road North and South.

Earliest Mentions

Wexford Corporation built the original Davitt Road South (consisting of twelve houses) in 1930/1931.

It was in 1939 that Wexford Corporation erected the eight houses of Davitt Road North. These would generally house 'retained' members of the volunteer fire service.

The newer houses of Davitt Road South and North were built in two phases in the 1960s.

Buildings

A new fire station opened at Davitt Road in 1940.

In 1970, ten days after tenants moved in, electricity was connected to Kennedy Park and Davitt Road houses.

People and Events

For houses at Davitt Road and William Street, the cost of Gas Company piping for six lights per house was £1, after base pipes were laid in 1939. The names of people applying for Corporation houses were published in the newspaper, as were details of how the councillors voted on the allocation.

The St Iberius parochial school moved to Davitt Road in 1965.

Other

Prior to the erection of the later phase of Davitt Road South, the land was open and marshy and part of it was a favourite shortcut for pupils from the south-west area of town heading to school in the CBS in Georges Street.

There are some tales of people searching for leprechauns in the area after a stage show by hypnotist Paul Goldin in the 1960s.

College View was built in the area in the 1970s.

Distillery Road

Origins and Meaning

Distillery Road takes its name from the distillery that was founded in 1827. At the time, Distillery Road was much longer than we know it today. In fact it extended from King Street up to the present-day crossroads at Whiterock Hill.

Even in the 1960s the register of electors referred to Bishopswater as 'the new houses Distillery Road'.

The road was opened after the Rebellion of 1798 to link with the so-called 'Newline Road' that was built by the military to connect to Duncannon Fort. Distillery Road led into town and via King Street to the Military Barracks.

Earliest Mentions

The road does not appear on the 1649 or 1800 maps.

It appears on a map of 1831.

The earliest references to the road are associated with the distillery.

Buildings

James Pierce had outgrown his first premises by 1847, when he obtained a large 20-acre site at the old Folly Corn Mill and Maltings on the junction of Mill Road and Distillery Road.

When the Corporation built forty-four new houses in 1914 it was noted, 'Houses cost £10 more than those already built at Distillery Road.' These twenty-two houses were built between 1909 and 1911.

People and Events

In 1832 John Mahoney, Mayglass, was scalded to death in a wash keeve at Bishopswater Distillery.

In 1833 carts lined up here to collect grain for cattle feed.

Thomas Styles, who died aged ninety-six in 1884, had worked for thirty years in the Distillery.

Michael Meyler of Distillery Road was noted as a ship's carpenter in 1885.

Patrick Doyle, Distillery Road, a noted Gaelic footballer who starred with the Mulgannon Harriers, was one of the victims of the Ardcavan drowning tragedy in 1900.

In 1902 Henry Webster, County Surveyor, summoned Joseph O'Connor, South Main Street, for obstructing a gullet (gully?) at land at Distillery Road, causing flooding on the road.

In August 1902 Mrs Kelly, Distillery Road, came before the Board of Guardians with two grandchildren. She stated that the father was sick and the mother dead, and she, being old and in poor circumstances, could not care for them. She begged that they be taken into the workhouse. Mrs Kelly had carried the younger one all the way and would leave them at any risk. She said she was prepared for gaol or death.

The year 1914 began in Wexford with a municipal election, a major occasion as was obvious from the fervour of the inhabitants. The aftermath of the election, on the night of 24 January, saw the town ablaze with bonfires. Beacons of celebration blazed from the rocks at Cromwell's Fort, the Ballast Bank, St Peter's Square, the Faythe, Patrick's Square and from the old Windmill near Distillery Road. This was in the field behind the CBS. It is depicted in a map of 1831.

Sinn Féin courts were held in Wexford town and in other parts of the county prior to 1921. In Wexford the judges were: the Mayor; Richard Corish; William Doyle, who as a Justice of the Peace had sat at Petty Sessions since 1901, and Edward Foley of Crossabeg. These courts were sometimes held in the disused distillery at Bishopswater

Other

The Bishopswater Distillery in Wexford town was opened in 1827. The capital cost of £30,000 was put up by two well-known Wexford landlords, Devereux and Harvey, who were publicly congratulated 'on account of their patriotic conduct in having ordered all the materials of Irish manufacture'. A spring known as Bishop's Well, supposedly blessed by the Bishop of Ferns, was the source of the water. The distillery had a bonded warehouse cut into limestone rock to hold 6,000 casks.

The Bishopswater Distillery produced Wexford Whiskey, and had its own cooperage and cart-making shops. The partnership existing in Bishopswater Distillery, trading under the name of Devereux, Harvey, & Co., was dissolved by mutual consent in 1836. The 'old-established' distillery at Bishopswater continued working throughout the Temperance movement, 'its whiskey held in high esteem'. Father Mathew's Temperance crusades significantly affected the consumption of Irish whiskey, although the four-fold increase in excise duties must also have taken its toll, and between 1846 and 1866 the production of spirits in Wexford fell by some 35 per cent.

In 1906 the Distillery employed fifty people.

In 1912, the lands of the old distillery were set for auction on 14 February. These lands comprised: a boiler house; an engine room; a brewer's office; the elevator room; a spirit store; a waterwheel; a still room; a corn loft; nine distiller's warehouses; a grain house; a gauging house; an excise office; a forge; a grain shed; a distiller's house and garden; a dwelling house; manager and clerk offices; stables; a coach house; a harness room; a cow house; a cooper's shop, and a racking store, all within half a mile of the town centre and covering over thirteen acres. There was also a bonded store at Paul Quay.

Duke Street (now Thomas Clarke Place)

Origins and Meaning

Duke Street was more commonly called Duke Lane.

Thomas Clarke Place is named for the Irish patriot. Duke Street was altered to become Thomas Clarke Street in September 1920, but withdrawn following a failed plebiscite in 1932. After reconsideration the name was re-established in 1981.

Earliest Mentions

It is referred to as Duke Street in Griffith's Valuation.

An 1809 advertisement refers to houses for sale at John Street opposite Duke Lane.

Buildings

There were thirty-two buildings here in 1853, consisting primarily of houses with yards.

In Griffith's Valuation the landowners here included: John Crosbie; Walter Eakin; Elizabeth Hayes; Hannah Myers; Eliza Atkin; James Atkin; John E. Hadden, and the reps of James Percival.

The present buildings date from 1969-71, and were constructed for Wexford Corporation.

People and Events

Elizabeth Roache had a school here in 1826 catering for thirty pupils and charging 'a penny halfpenny' per week.

Dwyer & Smith advertised themselves as 'bill posters, handbill distributors, town criers and general advertising contractors' in 1899.

The Faythe

Origins and Meaning

The Faythe comes from the word 'faiche', meaning fair green. At the time when fairs were held only twice yearly, the site alternated between the fair greens of John Street and the Faythe. The fairs were then the social event of the year and lasted for days.

Earliest Mentions

The Faythe is mentioned in 1540 as Ffayghtt Strete. According to Hore, in 1578 Kilcloggan held a farm of twenty-four burgages in the street called Fayght Street.

The suburbs of Wexford in 1659 were Faigh (the Faythe), Bridstreete (Bride Street), St John Streete (John Street), Weststreete (Westgate) and Maudlintown.

Amyas Griffith, in 1764, refers to a broad street about a mile long called the Fierth, but pronounced Faith.

In 1834 it was described as a long, poor suburb chiefly inhabited by fishermen.

Buildings

In such a large street, with its long history, there is a wide variety of buildings, the origins of which range over a lengthy period.

In 1764 the cabins were reported as, 'snug, with dwellers the most industrious on earth, employed in weaving nets and spinning hemp'.

The Christian Brothers established a school in Wexford on 2 May 1849 at a house in the Faythe.

Bishop Furlong founded the St John of God Order of Nuns in 1871 at Sallyville. They worked at the hospital from 1873. They took over the school in the Faythe in 1875. It was reconstructed and enlarged in 1944-46.

The Faythe once had four public bakeries, including one at Ovenhouse Lane. Here

The Faythe, over a century ago. (*Lawrence Collection.*)

The Faythe showing
the Swan, an essential
part of that street.
(*Rossiter Collection.*)

the women could take their dough or cake mixture for baking at a charge of 2*d* a cake, or cook their Christmas dinner for 4*d*.

The schoolhouse of Hobbs–Hatchell was at No. 118 in 1853.

On retiring, many of the seamen of the Faythe area built themselves two houses side by side, one for themselves and the other to let, with the rent paying the rates on both houses.

In February 1914 the Corporation discussed difficulties relating to house numbers. John Street and the Faythe were said to be particularly confusing with so many families of the same name.

'In the broad of the Faythe, the Swan Bar opening today Friday 21 December, 'a new bar in an old house', prop. Danny Morgan', ran an advertisement in 1945.

Throughout the 1950s the trade of Wexford port continued to decrease. Trawlers became the predominant vessel on the quays. Wexford sailors were scattered to the shipping companies of the world, or were engaged in the fishing industry.

Some of the men donated a statue of Our Lady, Queen of the Sea, to the St John of God School in the Faythe in 1954. The statute looks out on the lower harbour area, and perhaps echoes the purpose of the old St Michael's of Feagh church, which their Viking ancestors had viewed as they departed from or arrived at 'Weissfiord'.

The houses of Swan View date from the mid-1800s.

The Swan is a picturesque fountain that was installed in around 1888 by Robert Stafford, Mayor of Wexford, following sponsorship by Mrs Elizabeth 'Lady Dane' Dean Morgan of Ardcandrisk House on behalf of the County Wexford Society for the Prevention of Cruelty to Animals.

In Griffith's Valuation the main landowners listed include: William Furlong; Anne Carty; Jane C. Boyce; Joseph Pettit; Sir William Geary; Thomas Stafford; Nicholas Whitty; reps of James Talbot; James Roche; Ellen Rossiter; Robert Sinnott; Catherine Furlong; Catherine Dunphy; Jane Batt; Nicholas Murphy; Mary Walsh; Mary Codd; John Breen; Thomas Reville; Simon Lambert; Michael Murphy; John Connors; Robert Sparrow; Mary Ormonde; James Keating; James Codd; Patrick Rowe; Mary Hobbs and Editha Hatchell; Thomas Connors; Mary Connolly; Patrick Marley; Ellen Boggan; John Cosgrave; William Furlong; James Sinnott; reps of Joseph Thomas; William Byrne; Ellen Sheil; Richard Howlin; Lawrence Crosbie; Ellen English; Patrick Fortune; Patrick Morris; Anne Hearne; William Cahill, and Reverend George Whitty.

John Wall and John Clancy each occupied offices and ropewalks. Mary Hobbs and Editha Hatchell appeared as joint owners and their land included the site of the school.

People and Events

In 1690 Thomas Knox, a descendant of the religious reformer John Knox, became Governor of Wexford. He later invited the first Huguenots to Wexford. These refugees from religious persecution settled in the Faythe area of the town.

The Faythe was said to have been the scene of some great hurling matches between

The Faythe on a summer's day, as the ladies stride out past F. O'Rourke's and two men chat at the door of Tommy Kelly's Pub. (*Dominic Kiernan Collection.*)

The Faythe, near the entrance to Ovenhouse Lane. Note the low-slung prams of the day. (*Dominic Kiernan Collection.*)

the years 1750 and 1785.

John Cosgrove had a school in the Faythe in 1826, with fifty-five pupils at 3*d* per week, while James Carty educated thirty others, charging 6¼*d* per week.

William Whitty, a grain merchant of the Faythe, was elected Wexford's first Catholic Mayor in 1833.

In 1843, Nicholas Campbell is noted as a rope-maker in the Faythe.

In 1850 there was no enclosed fair green in Wexford and animals were bought and sold on the streets near the quays or in the Faythe.

Councillor Robert Stafford was elected Mayor of Wexford in January 1851. Mr Stafford was a generous man and his gifts to the people in his district included a fountain in the Faythe and four beautiful lamps for use outside Bride Street church.

In the *Wexford Almanac*, we find a reference to a boy named Murphy from the Faythe, who was in 1858 dying of hydrophobia, which was a symptom of rabies.

Captains Walter Bent Maudlintown and Joseph Rossiter, the Faythe, made donations to the CBS in 1859.

In an article regarding Corporation leases in the eighteenth century, the authorities recommend ejectment in the title to be served for the Butts or Rock of the Faythe, now in the possession of Mr Richard Sparrow.

All cordage and ropes for the port were made locally and there were two main ropewalks in Wexford. The biggest was in the Faythe. The Faythe rope-makers were Johnny Walsh and The Coady (*sic*) family, who were reputed to be related to Buffalo Bill Cody.

Two large fishing boats, the property of Mrs Devereux of the Faythe, were wrecked on the Long Bank in 1877.

In 1889 Mary Ann Neil's licensed premises in the Faythe was entered via a window in the back pantry. Constables Willis and Geraty later arrested a man.

In 1902 the Medical Superintendent reported on the sanitary state of the town. A case of enteric fever in the Faythe was removed to the Fever Hospital and precautions were taken to prevent the spread of infection.

William and Martin Blake, the Faythe, were among those who died in the Ardcavan tragedy of 14 September 1900. Martin Blake was a sailor, who had sailed around the world only to drown in his native harbour. William had worked in Howard Rowe's mill all his life, and was highly esteemed by his colleagues.

James Larkin addressed the foundry workers of Wexford in the Faythe on 9 September 1911.

In January 1912 James Connolly arrived in Wexford to negotiate on behalf of the workers involved in the Lockout. An arrangement was made and the workers were permitted to join a union, although not the union of their original choice. Work was resumed in February, but the bitterness and distrust that was built up in 1911 took many years to eradicate. Despite assurances of no victimisation, many who had given half a lifetime to those foundries never worked in them again. Connolly declared the end of Lockout in the Faythe on 9 February 1912.

News of the loss of the Canadian and Pacific Company steamship *Empress of Ireland* caused shock throughout the town in 1914. A number of Wexfordmen were among her crew. Thankfully, later news proved gratifying. Charles McDonald of the Faythe (who was fourth engineer), Robert Saunders (master-at-arms) and Frank Wadding (also of the Faythe) were among the rescued.

Lieutenant W.H. O'Keefe of Faythe House was reported killed in action at the age of twenty-one in 1917.

In 1939 the operetta *Kristine* by pupils of St John of God, the Faythe, was staged at the Capitol in aid of the foreign missions, admission 1*s*.

Alderman James Sinnott, who was first elected Mayor of Wexford in 1945 following the death of the then Mayor Alderman Richard Corish, was born at No.35 the Faythe in 1896.

Other
The Faythe has always been a community of seafarers. Until recently a ship in

a bottle would be placed in the windows of seafarers, especially lightship men. Practically every house in the Faythe and William Street exhibited one with pride. The Faythe was also probably the market garden of the town. The gardens belonged mostly to houses occupied by families of seafarers and were 'cultivated on the French principle, which admits of no waste'.

In a survey of 1886/1887 to determine burial grounds needs, the following was uncovered. Two hundred and eighty-two people died in the year up to March 1887 (or 23.2 per 1000 of population). The Faythe and Maudlintown were stated to be the worst affected areas due to overcrowding.

Sailors showing signs of leprosy were once housed in a cell in the Faythe.

People in the Faythe were fined in 1903 for allowing donkeys to wander.

The Faythe Harriers were originally called Mulgannon Harriers.

The Presentation Nuns were established at Wexford on 2 October 1818. A bequest of £1,600 from Mr Carroll of the Faythe allowed Bishop Ryan to secure the first superior, Mother De Sales Devereux of Wexford.

Rivalries existed between areas of the town, and natives of the Faythe were often called 'The Faythe Rays', referring to fish fit only to be thrown overboard. 'The Faythe Hessians' was an alternative nickname. The Hessians were a German mercenary force that was brought to Ireland from Cassel Hesse. They are remembered for their cruelty during the 1798 Rebellion and may have been stationed for a time at the Old Barracks.

'The Faythe Fishing Craft'

Midst the loud crashing elements' dreadful commotion,
These two Wexford skiffs braved the horror of the ocean,
In viewing our friends to their shattered skiff clinging,
A big breaker came, dire death with it bringing.
Brave Roche, 'ere going down waved a long, long adieu
Home to their families, their bodies were drew.
There was Roche, who from childhood the seas had been roaming;
Then Clarke, Brien and Campbell, alas, they're no more,
Their bodies were found when the storm ceased foaming,
Thrown up on the breakers on Blackwater's shore
Think of the Faythemen that are now in a tomb.

The deaths referred to in this Wexford ballad took place in a storm off Blackwater on 19 December 1833.

Fishers Row

Origins and Meaning

Fishers Row was most likely named after the profession of many residents of the street.

Earliest Mentions

One of the earliest references to Fishers Row was in 1833, when on 18 May a notice was published, 'Improvements proceeding on quay, beyond Crescent, line extends beyond Mr White's Castle as far as Fishers Row. A road is to be formed to the quay, to give entry to the people from Forth and Bargy.'

Prior to the reclamation of the lands on which Trinity Street and William Street stand, Fishers Row would have given access from the Faythe on to the harbour.

Buildings

The south side of Fishers Row is the older section.

In Griffith's Valuation the principal owners of land included: James Kelly; Catherine Kelly; James Sinnott; Susan Hughes; Mary Hobbs; Editha Hatchell; Ellen Clooney; William T. Rossiter; Catherine Murphy; Denis Carroll, and Catherine Doyle.

The corporation built twenty-six houses here in between 1969 and 1971.

People and Events

At the lower end of Fishers Row was a hall operated by Frank Swan and his brother. This hall was used by local drama groups for staging plays. A Mister Hanton was one of the local actors. The hall also hosted shows by travelling groups.

Mr French who lived in the street is said to have built a submarine at the quay.

Fortunes were well-known musicians in the area.

Other

In 1875, on 22 February, Thomas Brien of Fishers Row was born to Silvester (sic) Brien and Eliza (née Doyle). His father's profession was noted as fisherman.

On 1 March 1875, Jane Corish of Fishers Row was born to Martin Corish and Catherine (née Devereux). Her father's profession was labourer.

Francis Street showing Rose Terrace on the left. (*Dominic Kiernan Collection.*)

Francis Street

Origins and Meaning

Francis Street is named after the Franciscan Order, whose church stood on the corner of this and School Street for almost a millennium.

It was called James Street in the 1800s.

Earliest Mentions

The name James Street was designated until after 1840.

Buildings

A number of the houses date from the 1850s.

The Presentation Nuns opened their convent at Francis Street on 2 October 1818 with the assistance of their benefactor, Mr Carroll of the Faythe. It was established by Mother De Sales Devereux and Sister Mary John Baptist Frayne. Later, a private chapel block was sponsored by Mary Teresa Talbot, Countess of Shrewsbury, originally of Talbot Hall, together with a substantial wing built to designs prepared by William Hague. They opened a school for the girls of the town and also

Francis Street, with the St Vincent de Paul building prominent. (*Dominic Kiernan Collection.*)

undertook the education of the children of the Talbot Orphanage at Summerhill.

In 1826 the Presentation School was listed as having 180 pupils at Rose Rock. It was said to be operated by Mrs Frayne and four ladies of the Presentation Order (the former was probably Sister Mary). The school was free with expenses paid by the Lancastrian Committee.

The chapel of the convent was used for public Masses from 1826 to 1858.

The Temperance Movement built the current St Vincent de Paul Hall. One member was D'Arcy McGee, who came from nearby Paradise Row. In Griffith's Valuation the occupier of the Temperance Hall and yard is given as Richard Aylward. In the census of 1911 the Temperance Hall was at Francis Street.

Still Lane connected Francis Street to Spafield House. This has been replaced by a housing estate with an entrance between Rose Rock House and Hollyville House.

There was an animal pound here in 1853.

An integral part of Francis Street is Rose Terrace – a name often forgotten by locals. These are the houses on the north side, with railings and small gardens. They date from about 1825.

Roserock Terrace forms part of the street as it rounds the bend into Waterloo Road. Roserock House is conjectured to have originally been a foreman's house during the construction of the twin churches in the 1850s, and to have been substantially enlarged some decades later.

In Griffith's Valuation the principal landowners are: Lawrence Roche; Michael Finn; John E. Hadden; James and Eliza Atkin; Hanna Myers; Walter Eakin, and Thomas Redmond.

People and Events

Richard Aylward had a school at Francis Street in 1856.

The grounds of the Friary church were popular during the late eighteenth and early nineteenth centuries as an area to stroll. It was common for the townspeople to gather there on Sundays to listen to discourses of the then parish priest, Fr John Corrin, who, it is said, sat under the shade of an old chestnut tree.

In 1917 Charles Delaney of Francis Street was charged with playing pitch and toss.

Wexford presidium of the Legion of Mary started at Francis Street in May 1934.

Other

The Franciscan Order ministered to the spiritual needs of the Wexford flock from 1240 until the early twenty-first century. In times of persecution they lived as ordinary citizens in the homes of the faithful and ministered in secret. A brief respite in 1553, when Queen Mary was on the throne, saw the Friars back in their church thanks to the generosity of Paul Turner, a local businessman. Such relief was short-lived, and with the start of Elizabeth's reign, secret celebrations of Mass in ruined churches and Mass houses again became the lot of friars and flock. When the anti-Catholic laws were slightly relaxed, the Friars returned to their church (which had been built outside the old walls, near Mary's Gate). It was around this time that the brown habit was adopted by the Order and it became a familiar sight on Wexford streets.

George Street

Origins and Meaning

This street was officially renamed Oliver Plunkett Street following a Borough Council decision of 1920, but a plebiscite taken in 1932 to legalise this decision was not passed and the change could not be legalised. In 1981 a further decision was to make the alteration but as the majority of residents disagreed the old name was retained.

Georges Street is probably named after St George, rather than any of the kings of that name.

Earliest Mentions

The name begins to appear after the Cromwellian settlement.

George Street at the corner with Selskar. The present Greenacres replaced this building. The cast-iron bollard at the corner was to protect the walls from carriage wheels. (*O'Connor Collection.*)

Mount George, the home Dr Toddy Pierce, who was usually known simply as Dr Toddy. There was a great orchard here and pupils of George Street CBS would call to the back door to buy apples. (*Dominic Kiernan Collection.*)

George Street, showing the Gem. (*Dominic Kiernan Collection.*)

George Street, showing the old steps and boot scrapers. (*Rossiter Collection.*)

Buildings

George Street had many old townhouses of the gentry, such as Colcough's and Harvey's.

In 1809, 85ft of frontage was in the possession of John Sinnott, brewer.

Colcoughs of Tintern had their townhouse beside the entrance to White's Hotel. They had a theatre in the attic where visiting actors and singers performed.

A Constabulary Barracks was at No. 5 in 1853, it was still there in 1914. It later became Miss O'Brien's Girls' School.

The Christian Brothers' Primary School opened for the reception of boys on 1 October 1853. Friends of the greatly regretted Very Revd Dr Sinnott erected it as a testimonial to the pastor, who was Vicar General of the diocese. It had always been the desire of Dr Sinnott that there should be a school for boys at this end of the town. It closed in 1971.

The Loreto Convent was founded at 14 Lower Georges Street on Assumption Day, 1866. It moved to Richmond House, a vacant hotel, within three months.

On the site now occupied by the houses of Mount George, stood the house and extensive garden of Mount George, which was built by Thomas Brennan, a kinsman of the Pettits of Mount Folly and of the Powers of Edermine. Mr Brennan lived in John's Gate Street, separated from St John's graveyard by the entrance to the old grain store of Devereux, from where a pathway cut across to the New Road (as Upper George Street was then known). This pathway was known as Brennan's Walk.

Mrs Brennan's health was failing, and thinking the proximity to the graveyard to be unhealthy, her husband built the house in George Street where the walk ended (alas, without effect). The Loreto Nuns occupied the house for a few years before they moved to Richmond House, their present Convent.

Below Mount George, on lands owned by Boltons of the island, Mrs O'Connor built the terrace of fine houses. In an article on Corporation leases in the eighteenth century, there is reference to William Bolton, a gentleman 'who holds the piece of land extending from Upper Georges Street to the West Gate adjoining the Town Wall, for which he pays no rent'.

'Jem Boyle's Gardens' bounded the north side of Upper George Street. The schools of the Sisters of Mercy and the Christian Brothers later occupied this site. Snowcream Dairies and the offices of Dominic Kiernan would later occupy the site before its redevelopment as residential units.

The Mercy School was built by Richard Devereux on a site donated by him to facilitate the girls of the area, as the Mercy School was situated at Summerhill outside the town and was poorly attended, especially in bad weather. It was also a very great distance for junior pupils to travel. The Mercy School was intended as an auxiliary to the school at Summerhill, 'the ever-charitable Sisters braving the elements daily to attend'. The number of pupils outgrew the school and a new school was built in St John Road in 1945. The old school was up for sale in April 1945.

In Griffith's Valuation the landowners included: William Bolton; Richard Devereux; Sir William Geary; Charlotte Powell; John Hatchell; James Waddy; Samuel and Zachariah Johnston; James Vicary; John E. Hadden; Villiers Hatton; Jane Boyce; reps of Colonel Thompson; Ellen Hayes; John Talbot, and the reps of Darcy Talbot, David Robinson, Robert Box and Sarah Hamilton.

People and Events

Robert McCreery was a coach and harness maker in 1782.

A letter to Cesar Colclough of 3 November 1821 refers to plan to open a passage or street between John Street and George Street. It was agreed that no obstacle be put in its way and damages of 1s each was to be paid to Colclough and Mr Bolton. A cabin occupied by Colcough's tenant was in the line of the proposed road and he was asked to have the tenant removed, as the Wexford Harbour Commissioners could not afford to relocate him. The letter pointed out that the road would greatly improve land value and was signed by J. Redmond, Chairman, WHC. Another letter refers to ruins of a malthouse at the head of Georges Street to which a Mr Lacy had claim.

The Mercy Nuns, introduced by Bishop Keating, established a convent on 8 December 1840 at the quay but later moved to Clarence House. They built George Street School in 1856. They also educated adults.

George Codd was a shoemaker in George Street in 1843.

Recorder & Vindicator publisher Albert Hastings was located at the lower end of Georges Street.

In 1856 the post office was at Lower George Street, with John Green as postmaster.

The first interment in Crosstown was Carroll of No.14 George Street.

A report of 1914 read, 'At Mercy School George Street, four-year-old girl arrived early at school. Warming herself at fire, dress ignited, badly burned, removed to infirmary, died Thursday.'

In Red Pat's field, livestock auctions were held in 1918 and there is also a record of John Duffy & Son's Circus setting up there on 28 May 1923. The Abbey Cinema (originally to be called the Ritz) was built on the site.

Pawnbrokers in George Street were N. Tennant and Coffey. Davy Tobin was the best-known clerk at Coffey's.

During Feis Carman in 1917, Irish language events were held in the Convent of Mercy, George Street. Irish History was at the Christian Brothers' School, George Street.

Other

Old boot scrapers of an earlier period are still in evidence outside some of the front doors here, as are archways to stables.

Gibson Street

Origins and Meaning

This street cannot seem to settle on its name. Gibson and Peter alternate through its history.

Gibson Lane or Gibson Street derives from William Gibson, the former owner of the malt stores that dominated the lower end of the street.

It has also been referred to as Hay's Lane, because of the castle of that name that stood on the lower corner many centuries ago. It was said to be still extant in 1641.

This is one of the few Wexford streets where the later name (Peter's Street, from the parish in which it stands) is widely used and understood. It was officially noted as Peter Street on 1 September 1920. This was ratified by the plebiscite of 1932, making it one of only four of the nineteen street name changes of 1920 to be so agreed.

Gibson Street from Peter's Square with Peter Walsh in the foreground. (*Dominic Kiernan Collection.*)

Earliest Mentions

The town played host to King Henry II during the Easter season of 1172, when he is reputed to have done penance for the death of Thomas à Beckett in one of Wexford's churches. On 17 April of that year the king proceeded via what is now Peter Street to a ship wharf at the present Crescent and sailed for France. Before embarking he granted the mills of the town of Wexford to the Knights Templar and instructed the inhabitants to continue strengthening the walls.

Peter's Lane is noted on the 1649 map. It is named Gibson Lane in 1800.

Gibson Street is mentioned in 1764.

Buildings

Heffernan's, which occupies the position of the medieval Hay's Castle (extant 1641), has connections with the Hay and the Bolan families and dates from around 1825.

Wadding's Castle stood at the corner of Patrick's Lane (known locally as Foundry Lane). That castle was built by the Waddings of Ballycogley and was used as their town house. The castle was demolished in 1873 by Mr Wickham, who built houses on the site. Part of the castle was used as a small forge in 1869.

In the survey of 1662, a mill (then ruined) stood immediately below Mary's Lane, where it joins Peter's Street. Its corn stores remained the centre of the port's corn trade until 1825.

Bishop Luke Wadding's house stood on Peter's Street with its postern door opening

Gibson Street, showing the malt stores in the distance. (*Dominic Kiernan Collection.*)

directly backwards into St Mary's church.

Bishop French's house dominated the street at one time.

In 1902 William Higgins of Gibson Street operated a coach-building business.

In 1914 Liam Mellows announced that Mr Stafford was giving use of his Gibson Street premises for drilling of the Volunteers. Up to 200 were drilling three times a week

Lowney & Sons Furniture Store was in Peter Street in 1945.

In Griffith's Valuation the main landowners noted are: John Mulrooney; Thomas Redmond; William Swan; John Wickham; Catherine Connick; John Cullen; Villiers Hatton; Revd Richard W. Elgee; John Rossiter; the Earl of Kenmare, and William Gibson.

People and Events
In the closing years of the eighteenth century the Franciscan Friars opened a classical academy in Peter Street, the President of which was Fr Patrick Lambert, who was appointed first Bishop of Newfoundland in 1806. His successor was his nephew Fr Thomas Scallan, OFM, who was made second Bishop of Newfoundland, in 1816.

In the election of 1918 there was fighting between rival groups; Sinn Féin supporters were ushered down Gibson Street with a police escort.

In 1923, seventy-nine electric streetlights were installed. The generator was located at Gibson Street. The first electrician was Mr Wm Hughes and he was given a house at Ibar's Villas. By 1928 the ESB had taken over the streetlights.

Green/Thomas Street

Origins and Meaning
A map of around 1800 shows Slippery Green as the next road on from Bride Street. It was not built up at that time.

In a map based on 1812 information it is called Black Cow.

By 1831 there are a few houses shown in the lower end, with more at the Talbot Street junction.

Named after Slippery Green, or the street leading to Slippery Green, it is noted as Green Street in 1835.

Earliest Mentions
The sometime-name Black Cow, derived from the name of a well that was in

Green Street, shown in the middle of the twentieth century. The building on the extreme right became Bolger's shop, where CBS students spent their pennies on the way to and from school. (*Dominic Kiernan Collection.*)

present-day Green Street in 1840, in a lane opposite the school.

Buildings

The section called Black Cow had houses in the lane in 1880.

There was some discussion about building a technical school at Thomas Street/Joseph Street near the CBS monastery in November 1902.

The predominant buildings in Green Street are the primary and secondary schools of the CBS.

A dancehall was proposed for the area in 1947.

St Michael's Club opened on 1 December 1963.

In Griffith's Valuation the landowners of Green Street were: Charles J.V. Harvey; Richard Corish; Simon Whitty; Peter Doyle; Joseph Pettit; James Keelan; John Wade; Michael Murphy; John Guilfoyle; Jane C. Boyce; Stephen Keating; Eliza Codd; Hamilton K.G. Morgan; Tobias Rossiter; Charles Lett; John Dunphy; John Cahill, and Margaret Madden.

People and Events

Spouts were introduced in the mid-1850s at Green Street, Folly and Summerhill.

On 16 March 1875, Mary Connors was born to Peter and Johanna Connors of Thomas Street. The father's profession was given as a porter.

Reco Brothers' Circus was at Harvey's Field on 28 September 1947.

In May 1949, the Christian Brothers celebrated 100 years in Wexford. To mark the occasion 600 pupils put on a drill display at the GAA park. The boys wore white shirts and trousers with red ties and performed to the music of the Artane Boys' Band. At the climax of the day, the group formed the letters 'CBS', they then reformed to spell 'WEXFORD', and finally, white figures on the green pitch formed '1849-1949'.

The roof of the CBS collapsed at 10.45p.m. in December 1970.

Other

John Greene was born in Wexford in 1803 and educated at the Diocesan School in Spawell Road, along with James Roche (later Revd) and J.T. Devereux. He was then apprenticed to William Lord, printer of *The Wexford Journal*. He left Wexford in 1828 for Carlow, where he founded a newspaper. He returned to Wexford later and founded *The Independent*, supported by the local Liberal Party branch.

As proprietor and editor he was prosecuted and jailed for anti-tithe articles. In 1840 he was elected to the Corporation and represented Selskar Ward for fifty years, during which he was Mayor on seven occasions. He supported O'Connell and opposed Parnell. Greene was a justice of the peace and deputy lieutenant of the county but declined a knighthood. He was married to Mary Sweetman and had four sons; two became barristers, one a priest and the other a doctor. John Greene died in 1890.

When known as Slippery Green, the area was famous for 'The Slippery Green Fiddlers'. These were itinerant fiddlers who camped here when they came to town for the fairs.

Grogan's Road

Origins and Meaning
The name Grogan comes from the time of the Cromwellian settlement.

Earliest Mentions
Grogan's Road was called Bishop's Street in 1637.

The road is depicted but not named in a map of 1800.

Buildings
A Fever Hospital was built here in 1818. It had six wards and sixty beds. It was

used for cholera patients during the regular epidemics that visited such a busy port town. Bodies were stored in the Black Shed at the rear. In 1832 the Board of Health ordered the removal of a bed. This was opposed by a medical practitioner but police effected removal by force.

Liam Mellowe's Social Club was established in 1946. It is thought to have inspired the setting for Billy Roche's play *The Boker Poker Club*.

The site of the Fever Hospital is where the County Clinic opened in December 1955.

In Griffith's Valuation the landowners included: John Sheffield; Garrett Devereux; Tobias Rossiter; Eliza Furlong; Mathew Prendergast; Alice Lacey; Charles J.V. Harvey; reps of William Taylor, and John McParland.

People and Events

The Fever Hospital admitted 708 patients in 1843.

In November 1902 Patrick Kehoe, Grogan's Road, was convicted of assaulting and threatening his wife. He was sentenced to three months with hard labour.

One advert from 1902 sought, 'competent man to follow the Workhouse ambulance and Fever Hospital ambulance. Must be a good ploughman and competent to do general farm work. Wages, 12s a week. Aged thirty to fifty years and living near the Workhouse.'

In 1917 one of the regular entertainments organised for military personnel stationed in Wexford took place at the Town Hall. Among the artistes were locals as well as soldiers. Miss Doyle of Grogan's Road put on an exhibition of dancing, while Mr Anderson of the Royal Engineers did a recitation.

In May 1917, tenders were invited for the 'Colouring and Lime washing of the Fever Hospital'. Mr Kirwan entered a tender for the grass of the Fever Hospital field, but it was denied. The grass was needed for the Workhouse horse.

In 1943 creeled lorries loaded with turf arrived from the midlands for storage in huge dumps, one near Healy's of Alma, one near Wexford GAA park, and another at Grogan's Road, Wexford. In August 1942 two youths were sent to gaol for stealing turf from the dump at Grogan's Road. £5 worth of turf was taken.

A public park was proposed for Grogan's Road in 1947.

On Thursday 27 June 1963, John Fitzgerald Kennedy, the President of the USA, arrived by helicopter at Wexford Park. His motorcade passed through Summerhill, Grogan's Road, Roche's Road, Bride Street, Stonebridge, Lower King Street and Paul Quay, proceeding to a wreath-laying ceremony at the Barry Memorial on the Crescent.

Like tuberculosis in the early fifties, polio came under concerted attack in the latter years of the 1960s. Many people can recall visits to the County Clinic at Grogan's Road for the sugar lump, which was used to administer the oral vaccine – a major step forward from the anti-vaccination protests of the earlier part of the century.

Other

The cholera epidemic that struck the town in 1832 could be traced back through various ports to Bengal, India, in 1826. The Wexford outbreak began when two members of the crew of a schooner called *The Maria* died while she was berthed at the quay. The disease spread rapidly through the narrow streets of the crowded town. The newly built Fever Hospital at Grogan's Road soon had its sixty beds filled, as the ten doctors then resident in Wexford fought hard to contain the epidemic.

In the *Wexford Herald* of 20 November 1806 persons willing to subscribe to the erection of a Dispensary and Fever Hospital were invited to enter their names on paper at Mr Irvine's post office, 'As soon as 100 guineas is raised a committee will be arranged for its establishment.' Life subscription was 10 guineas or annual subscription was 1 guinea.

Henrietta Street

Origins and Meaning

The origin of this name is unknown, but it may possibly be related to either royalty or the wife or daughter of a principal developer. It was changed to O'Hanrahan Street in 1920 by order of the Borough Council, it failed to be ratified at the necessary plebiscite in 1932.

Earliest Mentions

Henrietta Street (or Lane as it originally was) dates from 1650. It would have then been a much shorter street.

The current street opened after the quay improvements of the early 1800s.

Buildings

The top of Henrietta Street is dominated by two old businesses (well, old by modern Wexford standards). Breda's is part of Hore's Stores, which dates from the 1940s when Johnny placed poetic, rhyming advertisements in the *Free Press* and *People* papers.

Alderman Richard Walsh, who was first elected Mayor of Wexford in 1849 and was returned to office in 1850 following the death of John Cooney, was a general merchant with a business on the corner of Henrietta Street and Main Street.

Opposite is Simon's Place, the rendezvous for operatic singers and backstage crew since 1951.

A sawmill was located on the site of the present mall, stretching from the Crescent to the arched alleyway. This location was convenient for the Deep Pool of the Crescent, where ships brought timber directly from the forests of Canada.

The building on the north corner of Henrietta Street is a lasting reminder of the value of our sea trade. This Ballast Office was built in 1838. In what was until recently our tourist office, the Harbour Commissioners met to rule the seaward side of Wexford, giving permission for trade, ensuring harbour rules were maintained, and employing pilots and police. The windowsills of the Chamber of Commerce building bear silent testimony to the mariners of old. There the 'old salts' honed their knives – essential tools of their trade – and left the furrows we see a century and more later. There was a large yard behind the building, where the essentials of the Commissioners' employees were stored.

In Griffith's Valuation the listed landowners are: Thomas Willis; Sir William Geary; Edward Goff, and Mathew Duignan.

William Redmond had a forge in the street.

People and Events

In 1823 Mary D. Crosbie advertised a house to let with yard and outhouses and a large gateway into Henrietta Street.

In March 1829, Mr W.H. Hyland was ordered to put Henrietta Street back in the order it was before being broken up. This order would have come from the Harbour Commissioners, who held enormous powers at the time. Hyland may have been putting in water or sewerage pipes.

The Hutchinson brothers of Henrietta Street owned the 'Reliance'.

In Slater's Directories of 1870 and 1881, John Bell is noted as an oyster merchant in Henrietta Street.

McCleane & Leary Coach builders had a coach factory on the street in 1880. The coach factory was just above the site of the present Citizens' Information Service. Older readers will recall the big gate and garden there. That garden was part of a lane known as Kenney's Lane that stretched from between Penney's and Hore's and turned into Henrietta Street at this point. The opening divided the coach factory from the commercial buildings at the bottom of the street.

People who lived in the street in the middle of the nineteenth century included: William Redmond; Thomas Willis; Mathew Duignan; James White, and James Redmond. William Redmond had a forge there but only Duignan, White and James Redmond are listed with houses. Sir William Geary owned much of the land.

In 1901 the street had eight houses of which one was uninhabited. In some of the others we find Thomas Hutchinson (one of the brothers) living at No. 5 and listed as a ship owner and agent. John Breen, a retired sailor, lived at No. 3 and Patrick Sweeney, a sailor, also resided on Henrietta Street in that census year.

In 1917 John Brown of Henrietta Street was contracted to carry out repairs to Wexford Bridge to the amount of £26. This would be the bridge at Carcur.

An interesting entry in the Harbour Commissioners minutes for 1925 noted, 'The harbour master reported an interview with the captain of SS *Blarney* and it was decided to put a full pane of red glass in the gas lamp at Custom House corner and a half pane in the gas lamp at Henrietta Street.' Navigation lights were used for ships entering the harbour and by keeping both lights in a straight line, one above the other (or as the old Wexford salts described 'keeping both lights in one'), a vessel came safely into the quays. Later, when the old oil lamps were replaced by gas, the leading lights were erected on brackets on the junction of the quay with Henrietta Street.

Other

Henrietta Street is interesting in that it is the last sloping street leading to the sea, moving south. After this all the lanes are almost level. This is due to the fact that the land around there was probably marsh surrounding the Bishopswater River.

One of its old sawmills gave Henrietta Street its more recent claim to fame, as the derelict building became a 'hippy hotel' during one of the festivals of Living Music.

High Street

Origins and Meaning

Throughout the British Isles, High Street has generally been the name given to the primary shopping area of the town. This does not appear to have been the case in Wexford. Although some businesses existed there, it does not appear to have been highly commercial and only gets mentioned as High Street in the 1800s. We may infer from this that it could have been a more geographical nomenclature, being elevated from the Main Street.

On 1 December 1920 the Borough Council changed the name to McSweeney Street. The change was not upheld in the 1932 plebiscite.

Earliest Mentions

High Street was called Upper Back Street on a map from the 1600s.

It was called Back Street in the early 1800s. This title persists in a map of the 1840s.

By 1883 we have the name High Street.

Buildings

When the old Friary had become ruinous and the roof had fallen in in 1620, Fr

High Street in the final years of the old Theatre Royal. (*Rossiter Collection.*)

Synnott rented a house in High Street, and built a thatched chapel on the opposite side of the street, on the space now occupied by part of the Opera House.

Bishop Wadding built a little thatched church in High Street in the summer of 1673. It was dismantled in 1692.

January 1832 was the opening date for the Theatre Royal in High Street. It was built for newspaper owner Mr Taylor. The new theatre, lit by candles and oil lamps, attracted huge crowds, with carriages clogging the surrounding streets on a regular basis. It incorporated an earlier terraced two-storey house dating from 1825 that had a square-headed carriageway to the ground floor. It was used for a variety of purposes, from a cinema to a circulating library over the years (see below). It was converted for exclusive use as a theatre in 1960/1961. The legend of the ghost of Johnny Hoey dates from about 1930. The building was also used as auction rooms.

The Wexford Opera House stands on the site today.

High Street opens out into Patrick's Square, which takes its name from St Patrick's church, the ruins of which stand at its southern end. The churchyard contains the tomb of the Countess of Clonard. The head of the 1798 leader Colclough, who was executed on Wexford Bridge, is interred in this tomb. His body was thrown into the river and never recovered.

Clarence Buildings were built in 1830 on the site of Bishop Caulfield's palace, and reputedly had connections with William Henry, Duke of Clarence (1765-1837), who was later King William IV (1830-7). Some time later there was a plan to sell the seven houses and garden by way of a lottery, with 450 tickets at £3 3s 0d each, but tickets did not sell and the lottery was postponed. Clarence House also had connections with the Redmond family who operated a tannery complex nearby.

High Street in the 1950s, with Stafford's lorry delivering coal. (*Dominic Kiernan Collection.*)

A bank of earth on the inside of the wall at Clarence House was thought to be of the Viking age but more likely it is part of the reinforcement of the wall prior to Cromwell's arrival in 1649.

Some of the dwelling houses in High Street, such as No. 13 and 38, probably date from the early 1800s, with varying amounts of refurbishment and reconstruction.

In Griffith's Valuation the landowners on High Street included: Revd James Hobson; Thomas Redmond; Revd Joseph Allen; reps of James Talbot; John Wormington; John Cullen; John Neville; Nicholas Keating; James Sinnott; Thomas Willis; John Rowe; Elizabeth Hayes; James Vicary; James Clifford; Charles Walker; Francis Howlin; Edith Tanner; Richard and Robert Allen; Mary Johnston; James Johnston; Richard Devereux, and Gabriel Rossiter. A large number of market stalls are listed, many classed as vacant.

People and Events

Sisters of Mercy came to Wexford in 1840 and occupied a house at Paul Quay. They later moved to Clarence House in High Street.

In 1887 P. Howlin operated an undertaker business from 24 High Street (corner of Chapel Lane).

Charles Taylor practiced as a solicitor at No. 14 High Street. In 1881 he invited tenders for a house at Rose Rock. Lt Atkin of the Royal Navy was living here in 1823.

In 1891 W. Andrews of 13 High Street advertised himself as a portrait and landscape photographer. His new studio was 'thoroughly warmed' and photos of late lamented clergy were available. On 29 August 1894 Edward Solly Flood noted in his diary 'Flo had photographs of dogs done at Andrews.'

Thompson Brothers owned an engineering company on the Quay. At the turn of the twentieth century they closed the works and moved to Dublin. They were the last members of the Society of Friends in Wexford, and when they left the Meeting House in High Street closed.

Denis and Catherine Kenny, a young married couple from High Street, were among the casualties of the Ardcavan Races tragedy in 1900.

A. Ebbitt [sic] of High Street paid 1s per stone for good quality berries in October 1902. Miss Fennell offered piano lessons at No.9 High Street in 1902.

In 1917 Stoker Michael Cullen of High Street was reported to be feared dead after a disaster at sea.

When a republican flag was flown from a house in High Street in 1917, it drew large crowds and a protest from the wife of a soldier. Other members of soldiers' families also assembled and were very vocal in their protests. The daughter of the house refused police requests for the removal of the flag, so her father was brought home from his work in a local foundry to take it down. The following day a large number of houses in Keysar's Lane, where families of army and navy personnel lived, displayed Union Jacks.

Other

The Theatre Royal in High Street was opened by Wm Taylor in January 1832, and later that year it was leased to Mr McGowan of Belfast, opening under his management in December. Mr Daly and Miss Graham performed but newspapers reported that it was 'not packed out'.

On 31 December *Romeo & Juliet* was performed by permission of the mayor. The performance was advertised to start at 7.30 with the odd note that 'bell will not be rung in future'. Box tickets cost 3s, pit seats 2s, and gallery seats 1s. In 1889 Miss Tellier's Dramatic Company presented *The Octoroon*.

For three nights only in 1902, with matinee on Saturday at three o'clock and with seats to be reserved for 3s each at Mr Sinnott's of 29 South Main Street:

The Original Irish Company will present the world renowned Edison Animated Pictures witnessed by the Lord Lieutenant, clergy of all denominations, John Redmond and 250,000 people at Rotunda, Dublin. Pronounced by press as Perfection of Animated Photography. Including: Life in Ireland; National Convention; Punchestown Races; Cork Exhibition; Spring Show; Little Tich; Tally Ho; President McKinley's Funeral; Across the Atlantic; Niagara Falls; 500 humorous, mystical and up to date pictures; Archbishop Croke's Funeral; Coronation; Stag Hunt at Punchestown.

Doors were to open at 7.30 and the show was to commence at 8.00. A note in the advertisement, 'carriages 10.15', reminded the gentry of when to have their carriages call back.

On 25 November 1906 a new comedy *To Marry or Not To Marry* with *My Grandmother* were advertised. Mr and Mrs Lacy of Theatre Royal, Covent Garden, and Mr and Mrs Neyler of Theatre Royal, Crowe Street, were billed to appear with some others.

In 1945 an advertisement appeared, urging people to, 'Do your Christmas shopping in Theatre Royal Café– wines, sherries, sweets.'

The Theatre Royal continued to attract thousands of patrons from all over the world to the International Wexford Festival Opera each autumn, before its demolition in 2006.

Hill Street

Origins and Meaning
This name probably comes from the geography of the street, the major part of which is a steep hill.

Hill Street was for a time known as Cabbage Row. It contained one-storeyed, single-windowed, half-doored, terraced cottages. As in the Faythe, the cottages had fertile soil in their gardens, and they cultivated plants such as cabbage seedlings. This probably gave rise to the nickname, although it may also have stemmed from the corruption of an Irish word.

The name was changed to Sean McDermott Street in 1920 but the move was not ratified in the plebiscite of 1932. A new development on the upper part of the street was eventually called Sean McDermott Terrace.

Earliest Mentions
Hill Street is drawn but not named in the map of 1800.

Housing is depicted on the upper south side in a map of 1831.

Buildings
The Infirmary was established at Hill Street in 1737 on the banks of a millstream. The buildings, including the doctor's house, were originally a terrace of private houses. Most of the leading families of the county were represented on the Board of Governors, which included Mrs Hatton, sister of Lord Castlereagh, in the 1700s, and later Mrs Deane Morgan and Lady Adelaide Fitzgerald.

In 1837 the Infirmary had thirty-five beds in ten wards. By 1875 it had seventy-two beds. There were forty-two male and thirty female patients admitted during that year.

One doctor who worked in the Infirmary was Ambrose Boxwell Esq. This information was noted when friends erected a monument on his behalf, stating his long service at the Infirmary. He died on 8 December 1821.

In 1917 the Infirmary was the principal in-patient centre for medical treatment outside the Workhouse. However, it was experiencing financial difficulties. A deputation met the County Council to ask that the annual grant be increased from £1,100, as it was not in keeping with the price rises experienced since the beginning of the war. Since 1913 provisions were up £154, gas £58, coal £50, clothing £50, and medicines £5. Also, prior to Dr Hadden volunteering for military service, he administered anaesthetics at £15 per year but it now costs £50.

In the previous year forty-eight operations had been carried out in the Infirmary. If these patients had been sent to Dublin, the costs would have been much greater. The average number of patients in the Infirmary at any date was twenty-two. The deputation reported that a bazaar had been held to clear a previous debt, but such a method of paying for health care was not the ideal. The Council complained about the Wexford District being expected to pay more while the Infirmary had patients from not only the town but New Ross, Enniscorthy, Ferns and Gorey.

The Infirmary moved to Stoneybatter as Wexford County Hospital in 1923. The premises then became Dr Furlong's nursing home. It was demolished in the 1980s and used as a Wexford County Council yard, with only one of the original buildings extant.

A new gaol was built in Wexford in 1812, at the corner of Hill Street and Spawell Road – now the County Hall. It comprised of fifty-eight cells and sixteen airing yards and served for almost 100 years. The male prisoners spent their time on a treadmill or breaking stones, while the females were employed at washing, spinning and knitting. The walls of the gaol were 20ft high and up until the 1860s public executions were carried out on gallows erected on the gaol green.

Eighteen of the houses on the north side were built in around 1897/8, with the even numbers being completed in 1915/16.

Springfield, adjoining the Infirmary, was formerly called Springhill. In the early 1800s Captain Hudson lived there. For a time it was the home of Dr George Hadden.

In Griffith's Valuation the landowners here included: William Stafford; Jane C. Boyce; Thomas Bent; Christopher Taylor; James Roche; John Maddock; Charles Hewson, and Edward Maddock.

People and Events
William Murphy is listed as offering lessons in Hill Street in 1826 at 2½d per week. He had forty pupils at that time.

In 1831 the attention of the constabulary was called to the number of bull and mastiff dogs prowling the streets, particularly on John Street and Hill Street. Captain Hamilton said many were at large without logs (this was a method of controlling animals at the time).

A well, holy or otherwise, was sited at the northern junction of Hill Street and Spawell Road. It is recorded on the Town Map of 1854, and was greatly resorted to during the seventeenth and eighteenth centuries for its 'sanitive' or healing properties. It is said that Dean Swift (1667-1745) and Sir Patrick Dun, eminent Dublin physician, frequently recommended visiting it for certain cures.

In August 1902 there was much discussion in Wexford Corporation about gas lamps at Hill Street and Roche's Road.

At 8p.m. on 13 March 1923, three men, Parle, Creane and Hogan, were executed by firing squad at the gaol in Hill Street, behind the County Hall, which had been commandeered by the Army. The three young men had been caught in possession of firearms some days earlier.

In a court report of 1939 concerning the death of a young boy who had been struck by lorry at Hill Street, there was a reference to playing 'span' – firing taw at ones in ring.

In May 1942 Mrs Elizabeth Shuddall of Hill Street applied for some of the £600 lodged in court as compensation for the death of her husband in an accident on the London-registered ship *Asherest*. He had been aged thirty-eight and was an able seaman earning £15 12s 6d per month including food and war risk.

John Street

Origins and Meaning
This street takes its name from the parish of St John. The church and hospital of St John stood outside the walls of old Wexford, situated at the right-hand corner of John Lane as it joins John Street. It is today marked by the graveyard in John Street, as no traces of the church itself remain. According to Hore, the Knights Hospitallers of St John were established in the town by William Marshal at the present John Street.

Earliest Mentions
In 1659 Wexford was divided into wards: East, West, South and North. As previously mentioned, one of the suburbs was St John Streete (John Street).

In 1798 Captain Richard Monaghan commanded the 'John Street Corps' of the Volunteers.

In his seminal work on the origins of Wexford, Dr Hadden wrote:

> From the Slaney valley and the West Country the trail will then have had little choice but to come
> north-about between the mountain and the Slaney River, keeping above the marshy bottom as

John Street *en fête*, ready for a procession. Note here the rough road surface and how little traffic there is. (*Dominic Kiernan Collection.*)

it crossed the Carrick Glen by the Newtown ford (now bridged), and behind the Coolcotts Hill to keep above the springs in the Farnogue Glen. So from Coolcotts Lane the road came down by today's Upper John Street to the market entry, now Johns Gate.

Buildings

In 1809 four houses in John Street, opposite Duke Lane, were to let with large gardens to rear. They were in the possession of Widow Rook, Thomas Lacey, Pat Murphy and James Breen.

Cooney's house at No. 18 John Street had its own chapel.

According to Hore, the street had six tanneries.

James Boyle's Ironmongery Establishment manufactured most of the pierced brass fenders and engraved fireplaces found in the older residences in Wexford.

The house at No. 80 was built in around 1918. Dempsey's had a millinery business here. Prior to the building of the house the entrance to the factory was through a gate between other houses. This house was thatched, as were most of the houses in John Street.

In a large house of three storeys with five windows across, where Mannix Place now stands, Mrs Dower made much sought-after black and white puddings.

On the south-west part of Lower John Street stood a tannery, behind the large house with the railings. Mrs Tighe-Kirwan occupied it. Formerly it was the residence of Thomas O'Leary, Town and Petty Sessions Clerk. The gabled house next door was the office of the tannery.

Opposite this on the east side of John Street stood another tannery called Frayne's. It was later the residence of the Richards family and later again the home of Mr

Andy Tobin. Mrs Frayne built the house opposite, now McGee's public house, for her manager, John Cooney, who became the first Catholic Mayor of Wexford. John Cooney built the major part of the house himself. His successor was Stephen Doyle, who continued the leather cutting and tallow chandlery, usually associated in those days with the grocery trade.

Stephen Doyle, who came from Glynn, also owned a premises in Upper John Street, now 'The Wexford Arms' and the house next door. Some of the prices in Stephen Doyle's shops, according to an advertisement of 1885 were:

> Teas of the finest Quality, strength and flavour, from 2s to 3s 6d per lb. Port Wine from 1s 3d per bottle. Sherry from 1s 3d to 2s 6d per bottle. Claret from 1s to 2s per bottle. John Jameson & Sons Old Dublin and whiskies of other distilleries, 14s, 16s and 18s per gallon.

R. & J. Hanton had a livery and undertaking business at premises in Lower John Street, now Redmond's Guesthouse. Morris's shop in Upper John Street was formerly the coach house.

Behind No.80 and No.82 John Street was a factory that manufactured shovels for the malt stores.

William Underwood, who was the building contractor for the Cinema Palace, which was opened in 1914, built the three houses in Upper John Street.

In Lower John Street, almost opposite the church, was Kehoe's sailmaking establishment. Jem Kehoe, who died in the 1960s, claimed to be the last qualified sailmaker capable of making a full 'suit' of sails.

John Street, seen with the iconic Stamp's Chipper still standing. Duke Street entrance is just beyond it and John Wilson had his coal yard behind the white wall. (*Dominic Kiernan Collection.*)

There were eight tan yards in the town in 1896, including: Mr Nicholas Kelly's, John Street, opposite Hill Street; Mr P. Frayne's, John Street; Mr Sinnott's, John Street; Mr O'Leary's, John Street; Mr Cooney's, John Street, and John Parle's, John's Gate Street.

James Boyle operated a forge here.

In Griffith's Valuation the owners included: Marianne Hagerty; Elizabeth Hayes; Thomas Martin; Catherine Sinnott; reps of Neville Jones; Robert Lander; Peter Hanton; reps of William Richards; Andrew Laffan; Jane C. Boyce; Patrick Freyne; Sir William Geary; Daniel Cosker; John Burroughs; Margaret Lawlor; Thomas Mahoney; David Robinson; James Ryan; James Clancy; John Murphy; John E. Hadden; Anne Murphy; Patrick Chandlier; Robert Limberry; Margaret Reilly; Thomas Reilly; Elizabeth Reilly; William Stafford; Anastasia Sheerin; Jane S. Clifford; John Kerevan; John Bowe; Margaret Dempsey; Michael Walsh; Timothy Kelly; Denise Dempsey; Philip Chandlier; Michael Doyle; William J. Rossiter; Thomas O'Leary; Nicholas Whitty; reps of John Cooney; William Stafford; Mark Devereux; John Crosbie; reps of George Jacob; James Atkin; Edward Neville; John Duff, and Lawrence Roche.

One is struck by the number of 'Wexford' names in the ownership of this street, in contrast to many of the others.

People and Events

In 1793 the fallout from a general repression hit the streets of Wexford. Two men were being transferred to the town gaol located at Stafford's Castle, Stonebridge, when a large throng of friends and supporters marched on Wexford demanding their release. At Upper John Street, they were confronted by a force of fifty soldiers under the command of Major Charles Vollatin. Vollatin went forward alone to speak with John Moore, a farmer, who led the group. Seeing a soldier being held prisoner, the major was enraged and attacked Moore with his sword. As he fell, Moore struck Vollatin with a scythe. The militia opened fire on the crowd, who fought back.

As dusk fell on 11 July 1793, eleven men lay dead on John Street, including John Moore. These were left on view for a period to deter others. Five others were hanged for their part in the affray, at Windmill Hill on 26 July.

A monument to the memory of Major Vollatin, who died of his wounds, stands at Wygram. An uneasy peace reigned over the next few years but tensions were growing.

Robert Codd registered a bank in Wexford on 2 October 1799. He was a member of the Le Codde family. A story is told that one day Codd was returning from collecting money through John Street near the fountain in Captain Chandler's grounds, when his saddlebags fell unnoticed from his horse. A little girl found this but she was attacked as she picked it up and a ruffian made off with the bag. It is said, 'the loss drove Codd mental, he could not run the bank, sank into poverty, lived on relatives and died without a sixpence'. Codd's bank had been located near Oyster Lane and the chief clerk was Richard O'Connor, who later became Mayor of Wexford.

Bull-baiting was transferred from the Bullring to John Street near the George Street junction after 1800.

James Boyle, an ironmonger of John Street, was listed as selling Swedish deal boards in 1808.

Paul McMahon had a school in John Street in 1826, with thirty pupils paying fees of 2½d per week.

In 1833, during the outbreak of cholera in Wexford, it was rumoured that the Board of Health intended to set up a cholera hospital in the house of a Mr Clifford at the top of John Street (now the two houses occupied by the Cannings and Crossroads Grocery Shop). One Sunday a crowd gathered in front of the house, described by the newspapers as a 'Cholera Riot in Wexford'. One article stated:

> … the report that the house was to be taken over caused a considerable sensation and the people who oftener consult their feelings than their reason immediately proceeded to wreck the house. The windows were soon demolished and but for the timely intervention of the Catholic clergy the whole house would soon have been laid to ruins. It was certainly injudicious on the part of the Board of Health to have selected so objectionable a place for the cholera hospital, knowing that the prevailing winds would have scattered disease all over the district.

In 1843 Tom Hynes, hatter, and Nicholas Brien, baker, both of John Street are listed.

John Cooney was elected Mayor of Wexford on 1 January 1850. He served in that position for four months and eighteen days, thus holding the record for the shortest term in the history of the office. Born in 1772, he was first elected to Wexford Corporation in 1847 and represented St Iberius Ward. A grocer and tanner, Mr Cooney lived in John Street.

Two John Street men held the first recorded picket in Wexford. John Brien, a cobbler, and his mate Henry Denroche placed a picket on Taylor's of the Main Street in 1852 in protest over the importation of foreign shoes. They were taken to court, but no local attorney would take the case for the cobblers against the merchants. Eventually a New Ross attorney took the case. The final judgement was that there was enough business for both imported and home-produced shoes.

In November 1903 a complaint was made that women from John Street were taking cinders from the Workhouse.

The Cock of John Street is a waterspout that was erected by John Greene, former Mayor of Wexford, in 1858. It was placed at the entrance to the 'Plots', open ground where Mannix Place was later built. A small stream ran down through the Plots and was then piped underground. It was formed by the overflow from John Street reservoir, which was situated behind the present fire station. It originally consisted of one tank, but this was later increased to three. The water supply from the reservoir was originally in private ownership. Householders were charged £1 per annum for water. If they were caught giving a bucket of water to a neighbour their supply was instantly cut off. This reservoir supplied the town until 1800, when the water from Coolree reached the town. For many years afterwards, water from John Street reservoir was used to supplement Coolree in dry weather. Some of the 1798 insurgents are said to have hid in the reservoir after the insurrection until they could make good their escape.

Wexford witnessed one of the largest funerals ever on its streets, in 1918. The death of John Redmond, leader of the Irish Party at Westminster, cast a black cloud over the area. Redmond was leader of the party of Parnell and had come closer than anyone to bringing home rule to Ireland by peaceful means. He was buried at the family vault in John Street graveyard.

Among the businesses that were listed in Wexford in 1930 was O'Byrne's, 10 Lower John Street, selling fish and chips, hot suppers, tea, coffee, Oxo, Bovril and hot minerals.

Other
Residents of John Street, with its butchers and tanners, were called 'Tripe and Onions' by the youth of the Faythe, who were great sporting great rivals. The 'John Street Stone Throwers' was an alternative nickname.

John's Gate Street

Origins and Meaning
The street takes its name from one of the original gates of the walled town.

Earliest Mentions
John's Gate Street was sometimes referred to as John Lane, as in the map based on 1649 information. This name persists on the 1800 map.

Geography dictated the position of the Market centre of Wexford. When the early road builders built their roads, they had to bypass Forth Mountain and the marshes of the Slaney and Bishopswater Rivers. Where these roads converged became Market Place. The Danes continued to use these trade routes, entering the town at John's Gate. The Normans further enhanced the importance of the Market by feudal laws decreeing under penalty that produce could only be sold in the Market.

John's Gate Street – the whitewashed houses are long gone. Note the shutters. (*Dominic Kiernan Collection*.)

John's Gate Street showing its former splendour. The whitewashed houses are notable, especially for the small windows under the eaves. (*Dominic Kiernan Collection*.)

John's Gate Street on a busy sunny day. The young girl with the bow seems fascinated by the photographer but her friends are too busy playing. (*Dominic Kiernan Collection.*)

John's Gate Street to John Street, with the graveyard wall on the right. (*Dominic Kiernan Collection.*)

And so up to the replanning of the town approaches at the beginning of the last century, the Market Place remained the traffic centre of the town, 'The country people entered through St John's Gate from early morning, their carts laden with produce, complaining about the tolls.'

Buildings

In the year 1732 a lease of premises on the left-hand side going out of John's Gate was made to Robert Clifford for the term of ninety-nine years, at the yearly rent of 5s 6d. The lease expired in 1831 but the premises did not come into the possessions of the Corporation.

Mary's Bar in John's Gate Street probably dates back to the early 1800s.

A dispensary was located at John's Gate Street in 1911.

Mr Brennan lived in John's Gate Street, separated from St John's graveyard by the entrance to the old grain store of Devereux, from where a pathway cut across to the New Road, as Upper George Street was then known.

Landowners of John's Gate Street at the time of Griffith's Valuation included: reps of John Cooney; William White; Marianne Jacob; Michael O'Connor; James Nestor; Sir William Geary; Richard Devereux; John Stafford, and William Bolton.

People and Events

'Charles Mullen, private soldier in Royal Tyrone Regiment of Militia was shot in hand and arm while standing centinel [sic] at John's Gate on 17 November 1806.' James M. Strange, Lieutenant Colonel of the Regiment, offered a reward of £50 for information. Mayor Ebenezer Jacob offered a further £50. The soldier's hand was later amputated. The High Sheriff and gentlemen offered a further reward. A subscription list for those adding to the reward was opened at Taylor's Printing Office. Gentlemen were reminded to pay 5 per cent gratuity for the poor soldier in Redmond's Bank.

John Parle's tan yard was at John's Gate Street in 1843.

In 1902 the Medical Superintendent reported on the sanitary state of the town. Dr Pierse inspected the premises of Mary Larkin at John's Gate Street and found the ash pit full, causing a nuisance and danger to health. It was to be cleaned within a week.

In 1911 a case was brought before New Ross Assizes by Mr Belton, whose car windscreen had been smashed by a stone thrown as he drove along John's Gate Street. Belton submitted a malicious damages claim of £15 for windscreen replacement against Wexford Corporation. The Corporation's solicitor offered £2 10s damages to replace the windscreen with ordinary plate glass. In the event, the judge awarded Belton four guineas, remarking that the townspeople would have to pay for it.

Playing handball on the streets was seen as a hazard in 1917. Plain-clothes constables were used to apprehend the culprits, among them Michael Grace and Laurence Kehoe at John's Gate Street, who were playing against the churchyard wall. Despite complaints that there was nowhere else to play, they were fined 6d.

Peter Boyle of John's Gate Street and Charles Delaney of Francis Street were charged with playing pitch and toss around the same time.

King Street

Origins and Meaning
King Street comes in two parts: lower, from the seafront to the Main Street, and upper, leading to the 'Cross of the Folly' at Tesco.

The consensus is that the common name of the street derives from the Kinge family, who received lands in the area in the early 1600s.

The official name was changed to Partridge Street in 1920 but again this failed in the plebiscite of 1932.

Earliest Mentions
A Royal Street was mentioned in Blessed Virgin Mary (Mary's) Parish in rolls of 1592. Tempting as it might be to see this as King Street, the evidence does not support it.

King Street is not shown on the 1649 or 1800 maps. In 1831 it is noted.

Lower King Street. Note the street light on the corner and the cranes operating on the Ballast Bank. The painted sign on the wall reads, 'Entrance to Private Bar'. (*Dominic Kiernan Collection.*)

King Street. This picture gives a dramatic representation of the flooding that occured here in the 1960s. (*Dominic Kiernan Collection.*)

Buildings

Hore wrote of the seminary in Michael Street that pre-dated St Peter's College, 'Upper King Street with houses on the west and large corn stores erected by Alderman Robert Stafford in 1870 cover the old playground of the seminary.'

Properties to be let in 1884 included: a malthouse at Maudlintown, a malthouse at Slaughterhouse Lane, a corn store and kiln at Lower King Street belonging to Robert Stafford.

There were coal yards here in the 1880s.

King Street also housed Jordan's Dairy.

The post office was located at King Street Upper in 1911.

A paint factory at Ropewalk yard in 1900 was renamed 'Wexford Paint and Varnish Company' by 1939. They manufactured Capitol Paint in a factory located behind the then Capitol Cinema, which is now occupied by Colman Doyle's shop.

There were two air-raid shelters built in King Street in 1941. Each could accommodate fifty people.

The Devereux family owned a large amount of property, particularly on the Wexford seafront. Most of the buildings along Paul Quay and Lower King Street were theirs. Another shipping family, the Stafford's, later owned these.

Nunn's staff called the malthouse at the top of King Street 'the Pillar'. Built in 1872, and possibly having connections with the earlier flourmill complex that was operated nearby under the direction of Richard Devereux, this is now converted

King Street *à la* Venice during the floods of the late 1960s. (*Dominic Kiernan Collection.*)

Michael Street, at the corner of Lambert Place or Bunker's Hill. (*Dominic Kiernan Collection.*)

to apartments and retains the old name. The malthouse further down King Street was known as 'The Fields'.

Captain Morris of Monck Street had a small schooner called the Jane Hughes, which traded mainly to North Wales carrying slates. Captain Morris later retired from the sea to open a public house in Monck Street and to build Leinster Terrace in King Street around 1890.

Many of the dwelling houses in King Street date from the mid-1800s.

In Griffiths Valuation, Upper King Street ownership is divided between: John E. Redmond; John Cody; Ludford Daniell; Hamilton K.G. Grogan, and Anne Roche. Revd Richard W. Elgee, James Lambert and Edward Roche owned Lower King Street.

John Cody was leasing a ropewalk and offices on lands of John E. Redmond, Wexford Corporation and St Bridget's Chapel Committee.

People and Events

On 7 March 1875 Francis Fardy was born at King Street, Wexford. The father was Francis Fardy, coachman, and the mother was Eliza Fardy *née* Pepper.

Mr Wm Murphy bought Miss Browne's clay-pipe factory at the King Street end of Barrack Street around 1889. The pipes were popular until wooden pipes became cheaper.

In 1895, Edward Solly Flood's diary notes that, 'Transfield's American Circus and Novelty Hippodrome came to Donnelly's Field, Upper King Street, Wexford. Their programme boasted: Little Tina, Infant Phenomena; Brian Kelly, humorous Irish Clown; Fred Poole, somersault rider; Jimmy Hewson, the Electric Nigger; E. Beppo, jockey rider.'

While digging to install water pipes under the floor of Mr Morris's public house in Lower King Street in 1903, the workmen uncovered two human skulls and some bones. The police did not investigate because so much time had obviously elapsed. The find caused great excitement. The workmen procured a box and soon reverentially re-interred the bones where they had been found. How the bodies came to be buried there was a source of much speculation. That the ground had been part of St Dulogue's parish cemetery was dismissed as being only a tradition. A more commonly accepted answer was that they were victims of the 1798 Rebellion who were hurriedly buried at that time.

In December 1947 there was major flooding at King Street. Many dogs and poultry were drowned in the flood. Horses kept at the Ropewalk were released to avoid drowning. The Talbot Hotel provided breakfast for the flooded-out residents of the King Street area. In the aftermath, thirty-five men working for twelve hours a day removed 800 tons of silt and masonry from the street. As rationing was still in force following the war, a special permit was received from the Government to supply 120 tons of coal to help dry out the houses.

On 14 October 1966 flooding struck King Street once more. There was intense rain from 7.45A.M. until 9.00 — A.M. , and the Horse River and the drains could not cope. King Street was flooded to a depth of 10ft in parts. John Small of White's Hotel offered to facilitate the victims free of charge, while Celtic Laundry also offered free service. In addition, McCormack's and the Wexford Timber Company offered free kindling and assistance with the clean up.

A public sauna facility was first introduced to Wexford at John North's barbers in King Street in 1970.

Other
St Dulogue's church and parish site has been overbuilt at the corner of King Street, but its graveyard still lies there, with remains having been revealed by excavations for sewers and foundations over the centuries.

Mary Street

Origins and Meaning
Mary Street was also called Chapel Lane. The current name is in honour of the Virgin Mary.

Earliest Mentions
Chapel Lane is on the 1649 map.

Raby's Gate was at Mary Street. It was finally removed in 1835.

Buildings
Some of the dwelling houses date to the early 1800s.

In 1882 the executors of Francis P. Howlin advertised four houses for sale at Mary Street.

Raby's Barn became a coal yard and later a slaughterhouse.

Wexford Wheel & Carriage Works owned by J.J. Murphy was here in 1945.

In 1949 Mary Street was the proposed site for a swimming pool fed by John Street reservoir.

In Griffith's Valuation the landowners included: Thomas Redmond; Charles J.V. Harvey; Thomas Redmond; Thomas Martin; Elizabeth Hayes; James Burke, and the reps of John O'Connor.

People and Events
In October 1902, on application of Annie Day of Mary Street to the Petty Sessions, two children named Brien of Wygram Place were admitted to St Michael's Industrial School.

Maudlintown

Origins and Meaning
Maudlintown is a corruption of 'St Mary Magdalene', the parish and leper hospital of medieval times.

Earliest Mentions
Maudlintown was one of the suburbs in 1659.

Just to confuse matters, there was a row of houses opposite the Distillery called Maudlintown in the late 1800s.

Buildings
The main built-up area of Maudlintown only dates from the early twentieth century. There were a number of scattered buildings along the main road on a map of 1831.

In 1840 there was a brewery at St Magdalene's.

In 1884 there was, to let, a malthouse at Maudlintown and another at Slaughterhouse Lane, both belonging to Robert Stafford.

The twelve houses on the left at Maudlintown – going from the Faythe – date from around 1900.

Brockhouse, who were manufacturers of springs and known locally as 'Springs', were located at Maudlintown in 1930.

A number of the houses here were opened in 1936.

In Griffith's Valuation the principal landowners were: Mathew H. Harris; Robert Sparrow; Mary Hughes; Revd William Hughes; Peter Clowery; Stephen Doyle; Mary Sinnott; Sabina Chalmers; Patrick W. Redmond; John D. Duckett; Robert Stafford; Catherine Murphy; William Bosworth; Edward Cullen; Mathew Tracey, and Jane Anglin.

People and Events
There was a school in Maudlintown in 1826. It had twenty-five Roman Catholic

pupils and fifteen others. It was operated by Ambrose Pettit.

A native of Maudlintown jumped from a stricken ship off Curracloe in 1842, but became ill on the road to town. It is said that hundreds became infected with cholera and died.

Councillor Robert Stafford was elected Mayor of Wexford in January 1851. Born in 1813, he was a very wealthy corn merchant with a residence at Rockview, Maudlintown. Mr Stafford was a generous man and his gifts to the people in his district included the Swan fountain in the Faythe and four beautiful lamps for use outside Bride Street church. He was a very able administrator and was highly respected for his impartiality as first citizen. At the time of his death in 1886, Robert Stafford was reputed to be worth £40,000, which would place him in the millionaire bracket today. In the business world he was regarded as being very shrewd, but he was popular with his large number of employees. He died on 9 February 1886, twenty-eight hours after he suffered a brain haemorrhage.

In *The People* newspaper of 31 May 1873 it was noted that Michael Ralph, James Morris and William Harris, all of Maudlintown, were fined for ball-playing.

The Wexford County Board of the GAA was formed at 2 Rowe Street on 21 November 1885. In 1887 over 25,000 people attended a series of inter-county club matches at Maudlintown.

In 1902 Wexford Corporation decided to try to obtain privileges for residents to be buried in Maudlintown graveyard, as town residents had no such right.

Henry Webster, St Magdalens, County Surveyor, summoned Joseph O'Connor, South Main Street, in 1902 for obstructing a gullet (gulley?) at land at Distillery Road, causing flooding on the road.

The *Menapia* made a historic voyage in May 1942 when she sailed alone, protected only by the tricolour painted on her superstructure, to Boston in the United States. This Wexford ship was so small that the tugboats of Boston harbour dwarfed her. In the month of her trip, thirty-eight British ships had been sunk on the same route. The *Menapia* made two other trips to Boston during the war, as well as to São Tomé in West Africa. Her captain was Peter McGrath of Maudlintown.

Other

The North-end Development Association organised a regular suburban bus service in 1962, bringing shoppers from Maudlintown, Bishopswater, Corish Park and other parts to the north end of town to do business. They carried 900 passengers on the first day.

Maudlintown graveyard has various cut-stone markers, said to date from between 1700 and 1925, with some reputedly pre-1684. It is on the site of one of the earliest surviving ecclesiastical establishments in the area. It contains the overgrown fragments of a thirteenth-century church, which dates from *c.*1250 but has been in ruins since around 1684.

The greater Maudlintown area includes a local authority housing development dating from the mid-1930s. The streets reflect the maritime history of Wexford and celebrate the connection of this part of the town to the sea. The names used recall ships of the town's proud seafaring past like Saltee, Edenvale, Hantoon, Antelope and Gulbar roads and avenues.

St Mary Magdalene's holy well was in Maudlintown. An annual pattern was held there on 22 July, but during the early decades of the nineteenth century the patterns became noisy, undignified occasions of revelry, and were prohibited by the local clergy. It was later revived and was celebrated until 22 July 1935, when the old Mary Magdalene's well – the well of the leper hospital – was covered for house building.

Michael's Street

Origins and Meaning
This name derives from the parish and church of St Michael, a patron saint of the Christianised Norsemen. The churchyard of the old church lies between Michael Street and Castle Hill Street.

Earliest Mentions
Michael Street was called Bunker's Hill in 1840 and is noted as such on a map of the period.

Buildings
Dwelling houses date from the late 1800s, but there are houses noted on the 1831 map.

Joseph Meadows owned most of Michael Street at the time of Griffith's Valuation; other owners included John Hore and the reps of John Hughes.

People and Events
Bishop Ryan opened the first Catholic Seminary for the Diocese in Michael Street in 1811.

John Sinnott was born in the town of Wexford on 8 January 1790. He was educated in Salamanca and returned to Ireland in 1814. Bishop Ryan appointed him Vice-President and Professor of the Catholic Academy in Michael Street in succession to Fr Richard Hayes, OFM. There he remained for nearly five years, and, in 1819, he migrated with the staff and the students to St Peter's College, where he continued as professor and lecturer.

Writing about the seminary in 1875, Hore noted:

> …of it nothing remains but the schoolroom converted into four dwelling houses with an entrance leading from King Street and to the garden on the brow of the hill over Bishopswater Stream. Entry was from Michael Street, then known as Bunker's Hill and opposite the high sandy graveyard of St Michael. Upper King Street with houses on west and large corn stores erected by Alderman Robert Stafford in 1870 cover the old playground of the seminary.

Mill Road

Origins and Meaning
Mill Road was named after Devereux's Mill. This utilised a watermill and is probably one of two referred to in 1377 when John Bonderan was appointed custodian.

The Folly is this streets's more common name in Wexford. Mount Folly House was located on the top of the road in the early 1800s.

In common Wexford contrariness, the Folly was the name of the Rocks Road, now Mulgannon, two centuries ago.

Earliest Mentions
In the map of 1831 the road existed, but only some scattered buildings occupied the Pierce site.

In 1840 the map shows the flour mill on the site of the present supermarket.

Buildings
Pierce's and Nunn's Malt Stores were the dominant buildings on Mill Road.

Mount Folly house was erected between 1815 and 1825. It is said to have connections to Mathew Pettit, a brewer.

Henry Hatton, Thomas Reville and the reps of James Talbot are listed in Griffiths Valuation in relation to Mill Road. The buildings referred to are malthouses, a corn mill and a house.

People and Events
For many years, Pierce's was a major employer in Wexford and dominated Mill Road for over a century. Its story, in many ways, parallels that of the town. James

Pierce founded the business in 1839, manufacturing fire fans called 'Fire Machines', which can still be found in older farmhouses. Around the year 1864 James Pierce was manufacturing horse threshing engines and they became so popular that he was obliged to seek larger premises. He moved to the Folly Mills where he improved on his threshing engines.

In 1856 he entered a contract to erect a bridge on the Slaney from Carcur to Crosstown. The engine by which the piles were driven was made at the Folly Mills. Mr Philip Pierce joined his father in 1866 in the management of the Folly Mills, which had extended into the Mill Road Iron Works. The Mill Road Iron Works occupied nine acres, most of it covered by buildings.

The commercial success of James Pierce's horsepower threshing machines was remarkable. In a newspaper advertisement in February 1868 for his Folly Mills Iron Works and Agricultural Machinery and Implement Factory, he stated that 1,390 threshing machines had been 'erected throughout the kingdom'. This use of the name Folly resulted in the road between King Street and Mulgannon being referred to as the Folly.

Mill Road Ironworks had a strike in 1889 when fitters refused to work overtime.

A major fire in 1910 destroyed most of the factory but it was quickly rebuilt.

There was some correspondence in the newspapers in January of 1914 about meals being supplied at a cheap rate in the factory. This was seen as a good idea as it would avoid those living some distance from work eating meals in the nearby church grounds or rushing home during the fifty-minute dinner break.

The factory was used to manufacture shell cases during the Great War, with a large female workforce operating shift systems. About fifty young girls were employed in connection with munitions work at Mill Road Iron Works.

Monck Street

Origins and Meaning

Monck Street takes its name from General George Monck, Duke of Albemarle, who was granted the land and the ferry rights in the 1650s.

It was previously known as Ferryboat Lane, from where the ferry to the opposite bank of the river departed prior to the construction of the 1794 bridge. It was renamed Monck Street in the late 1700s.

When Mr Neville proposed a second bill in February 1790 to build a bridge over the Slaney, H. Stanley Monck was added to the proposed Corporation.

The Borough Council changed the name to McDonagh Street in 1920. This failed to be ratified in the plebiscite of 1932.

Earliest Mentions

Monck Street is noted on the map of 1800.

It is spelt Monk Street on a map of the 1840s.

The Main Street was widened at Monck Street in 1861.

Buildings

The Georgians rebuilt much of Monck Street, with houses for the middle class.

In 1809 No.7 was to let, with a good stable and yard, furnished or unfurnished.

To be sold in 1831 were houses and ground rents at Ram Street, Monck Street, Wellington Place and Wilson's Lane. All were part of the estate of Maurice Crosby Harvey.

The Crown Hotel, a coaching inn, now The Crown Bar, was established in 1885.

The Saddle Warehouse was at Monck Street 1908.

Kelly's Pub at the corner of Monck Street was very popular with the people of the Selskar area. It is well known later as the Bohemian Girl Lounge Bar, in tribute to Balfe the opera composer.

In Griffith's Valuation the principal land owners here were: Mary Ann O'Leary; Newton King and Mrs Tighe; John E. Hadden; James Sutherland; James Sinnott; John Stafford; Revd Henry R. Harvey; James Colfer; James Boxwell; Nicholas Scallan, and the reps of William Taylor.

People and Events

Mr T.R. Burrowes opened an evening school in Monck Street in 1809 to instruct young ladies in English grammar, reading, writing, arithmetic, history, geography and the use of globes. The fee was one guinea per quarter and classes were held on Tuesday, Wednesday, Thursday and Friday from 4.30p.m. to 6.30 p.m.

Mr Cooper's Olympic Circus pitched at the corner of Monck Street and the quay in 1819.

In October 1902 Patrick Lyons of Monck Street was killed when felling trees in the grounds of St Joseph's Home. A tree fell on his neck as he sat taking a rest. It was emphasised that the Mother Superior advised him not to tackle the job alone.

On Sunday 6 May 1917 a meeting took place in Monck Street to formally establish a Trade and Labour Council (later Wexford Trades Council). From the Amalgamated Society of House and Ship Painters came P. Furlong, J. Goodison and P. Roberts. John Sinnott and Thomas Walsh represented the Carpenters and Joiners, while the Amalgamated Society of Engineers sent J. Kearns, W. White and D. Costelloe. Alderman Richard Corish and R. Crosbie attended for the Sailors and Firemen's Union, with P. Rossiter and D. McDonald speaking for the

Transport Workers' Union. From the Typographical Association came M. Martin, W. Curtis and P. White; from the Plasterers' Society, E. Redmond and J. Doyle. The Incorporated Guild of Stone and Bricklayers sent M. Lacy and J. Keelan and the National Union of Railwaymen's delegates were D. O'Byrne and Thomas Doyle.

On 7 July 1922 the first Co. Wexford Republican death of the Civil War occurred in Monck Street. The man, from Belmullett, was working in Wexford when he was shot.

Other

According to an 1831 advertisement in the *Wexford Independent*, 'E. Sweeney at the new Hairdressing and Ornamental Hair Manufacturing establishment at 15 Monck Street will enter servants' leaving papers and 1s on his books. Employers paying 1s can choose servants.'

Mr Hayden ran the Classical and English School in Monck Street in 1810.

After a fatal duel in which William Congreve Alcock fatally wounded John Colclough, Alcock's sister, who was engaged to Colclough, lost her reason and lived out her days at Monck Street. When she died her remains were conveyed to Clonmore for internment by torchlight, leaving her residence at ten o'clock at night.

Parnell Street

Origins and Meaning
Parnell Street is named for Charles Stewart Parnell.

When it first opened it was called New Road or New Street.

Earliest Mentions
In 1836 the Earl of Mulgrave, Viceroy of Ireland paraded along the waterfront, past the gas-works, up New Road to the Faythe and back along Main Street.

Buildings
In September 1902 Moran's of Parnell Street advertised their Temperance Hotel, with bakery, confectionery, fruit and a ladies' tearoom.

At the time of Griffith's Valuation this was still referred to as New Street and the landowners were: John E. Redmond; James Carr, and the reps of William Lee and James Quinn.

A chronicle of 1852 tells us that 'The portion thus added to the town by [John Redmond] is now both an extensive and healthy locality including in its extent Trinity Street, New Street, [later renamed Parnell Street] and part of William Street.'

An institution at the top of Parnell Street for many years was Peter Dempsey's. This was an emporium of the best of fish and chips, served in newsprint for takeaway and on enamel plates for those wishing to 'eat in'. Peter's specialty was pigs' feet.

A major claim to fame of Parnell Street in the late 1900s revolved around the main drainage system that saw the entire carriageway excavated to a considerable depth over many months.

Patrick Street (Square)

Origins and Meaning
Patrick Street, now called Patrick's Square, takes its name from St Patrick's church, in the grounds of which lie the remains of the dead of both sides in the 1798 Rebellion, dominating the south end of the square.

Earliest Mentions
Patrick Street was sometimes noted as an extension of High Street.

Patrick Street is mentioned on the 1649 map.

It is not named on the map of 1800.

Buildings
The Friends Meeting House was built at Patrick's Square in 1842 (on the site of an earlier meeting house that dated from 1746) and was established by John Deanes of Silverspring House. Its caretaker was Jane Jones. It closed in 1927 and was sold in 1928. It is a reminder of the Quaker community that was prosperous in the locality until the last of the Thompson family left the region in the twentieth century.

The building was extensively renovated around 1975, to accommodate use as a hall. The Loch Garman Silver Band currently occupies the building.

In Griffith's Valuation the primary landowners in Patrick's Street were: Nathaniel Sparrow; Sybil Chalmers; John Wickham, and Revd Joseph Allen.

People and Events
At the south-west corner of the Square, Erasmus Smith founded his school in

Patrick's Square, with a very important sign just visible on the left. It reads 'National School No.4 Wexford'. The structure in the middle of the square may be a drinking fountain from the days before piped water in houses. (*Dominic Kiernan Collection.*)

1824. It was part of the glebe of the parish of St Patrick. It consisted of a central building with two wings and it had two schoolrooms. It was supported by a trust set up by Erasmus Smith and voluntary subscriptions. The Parochial school had seventy-seven boys and sixty-two girls in 1824. The school moved to Davitt Road in 1965.

In 1879 the Wexford Union had committee rooms here. In an advertisement they sought a medical officer and offered a payment of £120 per annum.

Among the seven who died in the Ardcavan drowning tragedy were Denis and Catherine Kenny of Patrick's Square. Their six-year-old daughter Mary was one of those rescued. Two other children had stayed at home on the day.

Other

Edward Solly-Flood died in August 1896 at the age of seventy. His wife predeceased him by only a few weeks at the age of sixty-two. Florence, his daughter, lived until 8 November 1900. All three are buried in the Pounden plot of St Patrick's churchyard, Wexford.

Ram Street

Origins and Meaning

Ram Street takes its name from the family of Dr Thomas Ram, Bishop of Ferns in 1607. The family served on the Grand Jury and in 1789 Noel was nominated to the Corporation for the improvement of the harbour and town. In 1793 he was a member of the Bridge Committee and also one of the town planners.

In 1920 it was renamed Skeffington Street, Francis Sheehy Skeffington (1876-1916), a participant of 1916 Rising. This change was ratified by plebiscite in 1932 but many locals continued to use the old name.

Earliest Mentions

Ram Street is not included on the 1800 map. The quay development had not been completed at the time.

It is listed on Griffith's Valuation.

Buildings

The Georgians rebuilt Ram Street and Monck Street, with houses for the middle class.

In Griffith's Valuation the owners of land in this street include: the reps of Henry R. Harvey; Christiana Connick; Robert Stephens, and Magdalene Johns.

People and Events

In January 1810 there was a school for young ladies at the Corner House, Ram Street, supervised by Mrs Grogan from Bath.

In 1824 Walter Tennant operated as a pawnbroker in Ram Street.

The following appeared in a *Wexford Independent* of 1831, 'To be sold, houses and ground rents at Ram Street, Monck Street, Wellington Place, Wilson's Lane, all part of the estate of Maurice Crosby Harvey.'

James Doyle, aged twenty-three, Antelope Road, formerly of Ram Street and James Meyler, twenty-nine, of Selskar Avenue, were crewmembers aboard SS *Royal Sceptre*, which was torpedoed by a German U-boat *en route* from Belfast to Buenos Aires in 1914. They were feared lost for twenty-two days until news arrived that they were safe.

On 18 August 1940, three German planes attacked the mail boat *St Patrick*, which was sailing from Rosslare to Fishguard. A bomb narrowly missed the ship and strafing machine-gun fire fatally wounded Moses Brennan from Ram Street, Wexford.

On Friday 13 June 1941, the *St Patrick* was on a night sailing from Rosslare when German aircraft attacked from a quiet sky. On that occasion the ship was sunk by the bomb and machine-gun attack. The *St Patrick* was eighteen miles from the Welsh coast when attacked; twenty-nine people including seventeen crewmembers died. Among the dead was Michael Brennan of Ram Street, Wexford, son of the man killed in the previous assault.

Redmond Place (Square) & Road

Origins and Meaning
Redmond Place and Redmond Road stand on land reclaimed in the late nineteenth century. They are named after the family of businessmen and politicians who were the moving forces in the work of reclamation.

Redmond Place has also been known as Monument Place reflecting the Redmond Monument at its centre.

It is now most commonly called Redmond Square.

Redmond Road was of course occasionally referred to as the New Road.

Prior to the opening of the bridge at the quay in 1959, Redmond Road was the funeral route via Carcur Bridge to Crosstown.

Earliest Mentions
As the land did not exist until reclamation in the late 1800s, there are no mentions prior to the maps of that period.

Buildings
The Dublin–Wicklow–Wexford Railway reached Carcur in 1870 and four years later it was extended to the present station at Redmond Place.

This railway station opened in 1874. It was built under the direction of John Challoner Smith, William L. Payne, and John or William Wakefield, as Wexford Town Railway Station (North), representing one of a pair. Wexford Town Railway Station South opened in 1886 and closed in 1977. A wonderful canopy supplied by the Thompson Brothers Engineers & Contractors Co. Wexford, incorporating iron work manufactured by a now-unrecorded Glasgow-based foundry, still covers the platform area.

The station has witnessed the arrivals and departures of thousands in the intervening years. These ranged from high-ranking political figures like Michael Collins to the lowliest of criminals being transported to gaol. It also saw thousands of emigrants take the 'boat train' to Rosslare and new lives in England or beyond.

At one time the crush of people in the station was so great that admission to the platform was by ticket.

On the site of the present Dunnes Stores, stood one of the most prominent Wexford foundries of the early years of the twentieth century. Doyle's Selskar Iron Works opened in 1882.

There was a proposal to build the Town Hall on the site in the early 1900s, but it was rejected as being unsuitable. A swimming pool was proposed for part of the same site in 1947 but it was considered too small.

The Doyle family of Selskar Foundry built Auburn Terrace, the row of brick houses on Redmond Road, in the early 1900s and the family members lived there for half a century.

A cattle market was built on Redmond Road in 1955 and operated into the 1970s.

People and Events
It is said that as a young man John Edward Redmond watched the embanking of the quay, and grasped the possibility of applying the technique to other sea problems of Wexford. He reclaimed the sea marshes at both ends of the town and built the railway embankment. He extended the quay where the Corporation ended, enclosing from Paul Quay to Trinity Street. He built the great embankment that encloses Wexford's slob lands. He rebuilt the Dock Yard and realising that the future of sea transportation lay with steam, he built his own steamer, *Town of Wexford*. His last words were, 'My heart is with the town of Wexford. Nothing can extinguish that love but the cold sod of the grave. When that day comes, I hope you'll pay me the compliment I deserve of saying I've always loved you.' He died in 1863 and to his memory his fellow citizens belatedly erected the monument at Redmond Place.

With the passing of the third reading of the Home Rule Bill at Westminster in 1914, a massive parade and demonstration took place in Wexford. At the request of the Mayor all businesses closed at 8p.m. on Wednesday 27 May to facilitate those taking part. Bunting and nationalist flags flew from all buildings and from ships in the harbour. The monuments in the Bullring and Redmond Place were lighted and rockets and fireworks filled the air.

On 12 May 1917 a huge crowd of people, along with troops of the Munster Fusiliers and of the Royal Irish Constabulary, assembled at Redmond Square. The occasion was the conferring of the DCM and the Russian 4th Class Order of St George on Battery Sergeant Major Pounden of Enniscorthy. Pounden, who attended the ceremony on sticks, was a member of the Royal Field Artillery who 'took over the battery when the officer was knocked out … maintained the position, and eventually withdrew under heavy fire'. In bestowing the decorations, General Doran of the South Irish Command said he was, 'proud as an Irishman and a Wexfordman to bestow this honour on an Enniscorthyman'.

At Wexford Petty sessions in 1917 Michael Hore, a foundry man, was charged with making statements 'likely to cause dissatisfaction to his Majesty'. In evidence, Constable Merrigan stated that upon leaving the North Station at about 10.15p.m., he heard a group of about twenty coming along the New Road (Redmond Road). He waited outside Doyle's Foundry to observe them. The group in question was shouting, 'Up the Sinn Féiners' at a number of National Volunteers who were marching along the road. The constable said that this road was a popular place for local people to stroll and that these respectable citizens were disturbed by the shouting. As one group shouted, 'Up Redmond', the other responded, 'Up Plunkett'. The Justice decided that the charge was proved but as it was not a serious offence he only imposed a fine of 21s (£1.05) and not the £100 or six months hard labour allowed by law.

With the outbreak of civil war in 1922 the Wexford Executive Military, who were anti-treaty, took up position in the streets and approaches to the town. They took over Rowe's Mill at Spawell Road (now part of Redmond Park); Nolan's of Redmond Place, opposite Redmond Monument; the Custom Offices on the quay, and Walshe's of Glena Terrace, at the bottom of Hill Street.

Other

Redmond Place has often been the location for civic events in the past.

In 1963 the motorcade of President Kennedy proceeded to Redmond Place, where the President received the Freedom of Wexford from Mayor Thomas F. Byrne.

Redmond Road was where whole families went in convoy on Sunday afternoons with their high prams and tansads – the buggies of the era.

Roche's Road

Origins and Meaning

Roche's Road is named after Fr James Roche. He was the moving force behind the building of the twin churches in the 1850s.

The Deddery was on the site of the present Garda Barracks. It was here that some of the fiercest fighting during the Norman siege of the town in 1169 took place.

Earliest Mentions

The name of Roche's Road naturally did not come into being until the late 1800s.

The area is outside the town wall but is marked on a map of data from 1649 without a legend.

It is similarly noted in 1800.

Roche's Road, with Roche's Terrace on the left. The butt of the gaslight standard remains here. (*Dominic Kiernan Collection.*)

The road is called the Deddery in a map based on 1812.

Some buildings appear on the terrace side in a map of 1831.

In 1845 a scattering of buildings are present.

Buildings

Roche's Terrace is the highest of the three raised terraces of houses in Wexford, being about 10ft above Roche's Road. Originally there were narrow steps on the north end and long steps on the south end. The latter have been adapted to a ramp in recent years.

These houses, along with those in Carrigeen, were the first Local Authority houses built in Wexford. The land was purchased in November 1887. Philip Doyle of Barntown built thirteen houses in two lots. They cost slightly over £79 each. The designs were based on privately built houses at Trinity Street. The houses were completed by September 1889.

St Bridget's Centre was formerly St Brigid's National School for boys, dating to the late 1800s.

People and Events

In August 1902 there was much discussion in Wexford Corporation about gas lamps at Hill Street and Roche's Road. At Roche's Road the problem revolved around which should get priority, lighting the steps from Roche's Terrace or the churchyard opposite.

Polling in the Municipal elections of 1903 took place at the Tholsel and the national schools at the Old Pound – it was actually located on Roche's Road – between 8a.m. and 8p.m.

During the building of the Garda Station in the late 1930s, a large number of human bones were found, and reinterred at Crosstown Cemetery.

In 1963 Roche's Terrace, standing above Roche's Road, provided a vantage point for those wishing to see President Kennedy as his motorcade swept past.

Rowe Street

Origins and Meaning
The Rowe Family of Ballycross built a major portion of Rowe Street, hence the name.

Their house became the offices of Huggard & Brennan. A family named Walshe, one of whom married Dennis Whelan, manager of Redmond's Bank, occupied it in the interim.

Earliest Mentions
Rowe Street does not appear on the map of 1831.

It is listed by 1845, with a post office noted.

Buildings
One of our twin churches dominates Rowe Street. The Rowe Street clock cost £366 8s 5d from Timpson's. The church is built of Wicklow granite and sandstone from Park quarry. The railings were made and erected by Pierce's and were maintained free for over 100 years. The foundation stones were laid on 27 June 1851 and contained a parchment with the names of the bishop, clergy, architect and contractor. The joy bells of Rowe Street church were blessed on 19 August 1883. The clock was removed from Rowe Street church due to constant corrosion.

The Excise Office was located in Rowe Street in 1846 and the Inland Revenue was at No.7 in 1875.

In 1879 Peter J. O'Flaherty had his solicitor's office at No.1.

Nicholas MacDonnell, surveyor for the Irish Civil Service Permanent Building Society, and resident engineer of Wexford Waterworks, lived at No.3.

Some buildings on the lower south side date from the mid-nineteenth century, while those in the upper portion date from some decades later.

In Griffith's Valuation John Rowe is noted as the owner of the larger portion of the street, with Patrick Walsh and Thomas Willis owning individual plots.

People and Events

The Wesleyan church, of which the facade remains, was opened on 9 March 1863 with a congregation of 500. The first sermon was preached by the Revd Robert Newton of Manchester. The Minister of Bethesda church at Cornmarket declined his Sunday services at the time to allow people to attend and help pay for the new building, which was designed by Thomas Willis. The congregation had previously met in a house in Allen Street.

The National League regularly met in rooms at No.2 Rowe Street in 1884.

James McCarthy had a tailoring establishment at No.11 Rowe Street (on the corner of High Street) in 1903.

The Wexford County Board of the GAA was founded at No.2 Rowe Street on 21 November 1885.

A news report in 1917 stated that, 'as a jennet and cart, the property of Godkin and Co. was being driven up Rowe Street, the animal became restive. Despite the best efforts of the driver, the cart backed into the window of Mr Breen's drapery

Rowe Street, with the shops of N. Furlong and F.J. O'Rourke, as well as Sharkey's Hairdressers. (*Dominic Kiernan Collection.*)

establishment. The window was smashed to atoms.'

Vize Charles, a well-known photographer, died in a motorcar accident while travelling with Hugh McGuire. Both lived at Upper Rowe Street. His widow claimed £5,000 in the High Court in 1929.

The offices of Huggard, Brennan & Murphy still sport a brass plaque noting the 'Offices of Mr Huggard'. There was a connection between this firm and author John Welcome, who wrote thrillers, racing stories and much more.

Other
An article on court houses in Wexford refers to 'the general market which was held in the place now occupied by the Methodist church at the end of Rowe Street'.

School Street

Origins and Meaning
School Street takes its name from the fact that Mr W. Doran founded the Wexford Poor School there in 1809, on the site of what is now the Third Order Hall.

In *Sights & Scenes* there is a reference to, 'the national school for boys, situated near the Manse, or residence of the Catholic curates, in School Street'.

Earliest Mentions
The name School Street is not used on maps prior to 1800. It appears to be seen as an extension of John Street.

In 1843 there is mention of Redmond's tan yard in School Street.

By 1845 School Street is the official name.

Buildings
Lancaster House, once the property of the Redmond family, opposite the Third Order Hall, is named for a school that used the Lancastrian method of education. This method of teaching, developed by Joseph Lancaster, meant that brighter pupils (called monitors or prefects) were taught by the teacher, and they in turn taught the other children. This permitted large numbers of children to be educated. The method was widely used in Europe and America.

In 1888 the tannery of Thomas S. Redmond was in School Street. It was extant in 1903.

The residence of the Catholic clergy of the town is also situated on School Street. It was built in 1838 and is a fine example of late Georgian architecture. It is

School Street showing Lancaster House.
(*Dominic Kiernan Collection.*)

variously called the Manse or the Presbytery. It was built by Fr O'Brien originally having connections with the nearby church of the Immaculate Conception, but later adapted to serve the clergy of both 'twin churches'.

The building on the corner of Mary Street was part of the Redmond family tannery. It was here that the skins were dried.

The terrace of houses replaces a corn store that was part of O'Keefe's malt store, extending into St Peter's Square.

Old Pound House dates from the beginning of the twentieth century. It is probably on the site of an older dwelling.

The landowners on this street in Griffith's Valuation include: Walter Eakin; Charles J.V. Harvey; Mary Johnston; Sir William Geary; Revd William Murphy; William Bell; Mary Furlong; Eliza Furlong, and Thomas Redmond.

People and Events

John Cassidy and James Dawson operated a school free of fees and stated to be 'under clergy' in School Street in 1826. This may refer to the national school previously mentioned.

P.R. Hanrahan was principal of the Lancastrian School from 1831 until it was disestablished in 1878. He was a classical scholar and loved poetry. A collection of his work, *Echoes of the Past*, includes 'The Fetch'. The following lines of that poem reflect part of our folklore (overleaf):

School Street, showing the old storage buildings. Note the door on the second level for loading on to carts. (*Dominic Kiernan Collection.*)

> I knew he'd die,
> For the banshee's song
> The whole night long
> Was heard from the bawn.
> I knew he'd die,
> For the fetch was seen
> In the green boreen
> By the fairy's path

Mr Hanrahan died at Farnogue Cottage aged seventy-eight and he is buried at Carrig.

Selskar Street

Origins and Meaning
Selskar is one of the oldest parishes in the town of Wexford.

The word 'Selskar' is sometimes seen as a corruption of St Sepulchre, or Holy Sepulchre, referring to the abbey.

An alternative derivation is that it is old Danish/Norse meaning 'seal skar' or 'seal rock', referring to an outcrop in the river near the abbey.

Earliest Mentions

Early mentions can be confusing because the present Abbey Street was once referred to as Selskar Street, and this area is also called North Main Street.

On a map of 1845 it is called North Main Street.

Buildings

This part of the town proved very popular as a location for town houses of the gentry and many of the older buildings date from the expansion of the late 1700s and early 1800s.

In Griffith's Valuation the owners of land include: Walter Eakin; James Sinnott; Christina Connick; Nicholas Sinnott; Thomas Willis; William Byrne; Edward O'Brien; Emma Wheeler; reps of Robert Harvey; Robert Sinnott; Anne Redmond; William Armstrong; Christopher Taylor; W.B. Gurley; Robert Ball; John E. Hadden; John Walsh; George Armstrong; Robert Sparrow; Matthew McCann; George Talbot; John Richards; Ludford Daniel; Patrick Furlong; Charlotte Powell; Ellen Hayes; reps of John Talbot, and John Crosbie,

Richard Shaw was noted as occupier of a house, baths and garden.

Selskar Street, showing some of the older shops and the entrance to Trimmer's Lane East. (*Dominic Kiernan Collection.*)

People and Events

This notice appeared in the *Wexford Herald* in 1808:

> Just arrived in town, a person who can destroy the vermin called rats and mice. All millers, maltsters, corn factors, brewers, bakers, captains of ships, should contact him soon, as he will only spend a few days in town. Vermin will neither, eat, drink, nor vomit after taking this. Certificates from nobility, gentry, etc. To be seen on application at his lodgings at Mr Ennis's of Selskar.

In the *Wexford Herald* of July 1809 Mrs Montague advertised to teach, 'that polite language, French'. Applications were to be made to her house at Selskar, 'next door but one to Mr Richards, Attorney'. Mr Montague, meanwhile, offered 'to engage to perfect grown-up ladies and gentlemen in dancing in thirty-two teachings on payment of 1 guinea entry and 1 guinea for every eight lessons'.

Edward O'Brien operated a boarding school in Selskar in 1926, charging 2s 1d per week. He had forty-five pupils.

In June 1844, instructions were issued to George Little, solicitor, Selskar, to take action against the owner of the *Eclipse* Steamer for 'forcibly carrying away our pilot Nicholas King, to Dublin on 13 June'.

On 13 January 1877, Mrs Mary Callaghan died very suddenly in Selskar.

No. 38 Selskar Street was the residence of the Harveys of Killiane Castle. In 1798 Mr Turner was dining with Harvey at his house in Selskar when a mob assembled demanding his life, as Turner was a magistrate who had taken their weapons. After much negotiation it was agreed to have Turner jailed to await trial.

Later the house was used as a barracks for the mounted police. At the Assizes they escorted the Judge to and from the court. When Inspector Brummel of the barracks died, his horse with his empty saddle, his sword and his spurs, followed the hearse to the church and Selskar graveyard. Mr Lyons eventually took over the house and opened the Imperial Hotel. In 1881 Charles Stewart Parnell stayed there while in Wexford. At the champagne supper that night in the hotel the conversation turned to his impending arrest.

The Imperial was unfortunately destroyed by fire in 1983.

Katty Kane kept a shop at No. 94 Selskar Street. She was the last resident of Esmonde Kyne's townhouse. It was said that, 'She'd give you a halfpenny or a penny or a jam tart for a rabbit skin killed by a dog and not ruined by shot, or a coconut for a few of them.' Katty played the accordion and sang of Negro spirituals.

Kelly's Pub at the corner of Monck Street was very popular with the people of the area.

S.V. O'Connor, with a business at No. 14 Selskar Street, was an analytical and consulting chemist in 1902.

James Breen was an undertaker there in 1914, while F. Carty had an umbrella factory.

In January 1939 a number of pubs were prosecuted for having people on the premises after closing time. These were the Selskar, the Cape and the Imperial Hotel. Closing time on Saturdays was 9.30 p.m.

Bernard Fitzsimons, uncle of Maureen O'Hara, lived in Selskar and worked at McCormack & Hegarty. N.J. Cullen owned the Selskar Cycle & Gramophone Depot in 1945.

In 1966 Hodnett & Co. of No.36 Selskar Street were accountants, and La Tulipe was a popular hairdressing establishment.

O'Brien's furniture store was gutted by fire in January 1971.

Other

In 1793 John Elgee was appointed Curate of the parish of St Selskar, Wexford. In 1796 he was appointed Rector of the parish and so remained until his death in 1823. (It would appear that at this time the parish was known as the parish of St Selskar and not the parish of Wexford.)

Slaney Street

Origins and Meaning

Slaney Street takes its name from the river. Prior to land reclamation in the 1800s the river lapped the lower end of the street.

Earliest Mentions

In *A '98 Diary* by Mrs Lett we find this passage, 'Mrs Johnson's trusty maidservant sought her out, and came to induce her to return to her lodgings, which were undisturbed. Her abode was at a Quaker's in Slaney Street.'

Buildings

In 1809 a newspaper advertisement announced, 'Building ground to let and house and concerns occupied lately by Royal Artillery.' William Kellett of Clonard was the person to contact.

Similarly, in the April of that year, the *Wexford Herald* had an advertisement regarding the letting of Dr Johnston's house, with a coach house and stable adjoining and two gardens.

Stones Girls' Boarding School was located there in the 1820s.

Maria Theresa O'Brien charged fees of 4s 5d per week for her boarding school in

Slaney Street in 1826. She had sixty-six pupils.

The lower end of Slaney Street had the Artillery Park until around 1840. This is shown on the map of 1800.

There was a Constabulary Barracks in Slaney Street in 1846.

The buildings at the lower north side of the street are said to date from the late 1800s.

In Griffith's Valuation the landowners here include: John E. Redmond; George Reid; John Leared; Richard Leared, and Arthur and William Kellett.

The land owned by Redmond housed an auxiliary workhouse with a yard and garden operated by the Guardians of the Poor Law Union of the time.

People and Events
The families of Tuskar Rock Lighthouse keepers occupied houses in the street in the 1880s. This came about after an inspector, who was an ancestor of Winston Churchill, claimed that living on the rock, as had been the custom, was too dangerous for the families.

George Hawkins, lighthouse keeper, was recorded as living in Slaney Street in 1885.

In the record of Corporation leases of the eighteenth century we find, 'a lease was made of a Park in the Liberties of Wexford in the year 1732 at £2 1s 6d a year for the term of sixty-one years, which lease expired in 1793. Miss Clifford of Slaney Street is in possession of this holding but pays no rent.'

Other
Sand and gravel used in the refurbishment of Woolworth's shop prior to its opening in April 1952 came from F.M. Brady of Slaney Street.

Spawell Road

Origins and Meaning
Spawell Road stretches from Carcur to Slaney Street, incorporating West Gate (formerly Cow Gate). It takes its name from the Spa Well, which was famous in the eighteenth century.

In 1748 it was recorded:

> Near one of the Gates is a small structure that covers a mineral well, which they call the Spa. But the look of the water did not invite me to taste it. It was covered with an oily scum that forbid me. (Wells of some iron-saturated waters if undisturbed tend to acquire a yellow film of iron oxide that

Spawell Road, with a view of Howard Rowe's Mill. (*O'Connor Collection.*)

does not look inviting.) Yet this well is of some advantage to the town, for many resort there on account of the spring, though not in such numbers as formerly.

Earliest Mentions

The area was called Whitewell in 1650, according to Hore.

It was called St Brigid's Road in 1914, probably from the name of the home for inebriates.

Buildings

West Gate Hotel was established by Mr Richard McDonnell:

…who by a large outlay of capital erected a splendid hotel, which is situated immediately opposite the abbey [Selskar] grounds. From the front windows of this excellent establishment, the grand and picturesque ruins of the church, the castles and the ancient town wall are fully open to the visitor's view.

The yard opposite was the livery yard of the hotel. The opening dinner was held on 15 April 1856 with John Talbot in the chair. In 1873 Richard McDonnell sold the business for £3,400 to a number of wine and spirit merchants. The hotel became Walpole's Wine and Grocery. The livery yard opposite was a natural addition to the business, as the country people parked their carts there for Walpole's to deliver the weekly groceries. The license provided refreshments for the road, and the public clock on the wall was the weekly timekeeper for half the country. It was later Ryan's, then McCabe's and later Halligan's grocery and licensed premises.

Spa Cottage was occupied by Ponsonby Hore in 1824.

The Inebriate Reformatory was listed at Spawell Road in the 1911 census.

Spawell House was the biggest in Wexford at one time. It is now the front portion of Wexford Vocational College. Mr Harvey occupied it originally. The house was later divided, and George H. Jacob lived in the southern half. He supplied the official stamped paper for legal documents for the county. Dr Jacob was Mayor of Wexford in 1799. The larger part of the residence became the County Club until the early years of the twentieth century. The County Tennis Club continued in its grounds until it moved to Melrose.

At Weston lived Joseph Meadows, Clerk of the Peace, whose son Harry compiled the Meadows list of townlands, parishes, and baronies of County Wexford.

Fort View was the town house of the Sandwith family in the middle of the nineteenth century.

In the early 1900s the gaol was closed. It then became St Brigid's Home for Inebriates, under the care of the Sisters of St John of God, and the walls were cut down to their present proportions. Later it became the headquarters of the Wexford County Council and so it remains.

Beechville, which was later divided and renamed Elmfield and Rosemount, was occupied in the middle of the nineteenth century by Doctor Barrington's Diocesan School. Some blank windows are reminders of the 'Window Tax'.

Its gardens and playing fields offered a public promenade at the end of the eighteenth century. During a quarrel over tolls between the Bridge Company and the Military, Col. Wygram brought his regimental bands to play here, and the townspeople forsook the bridge for what was known as the 'green walks'. Due to the loss of income from the reduced tolls, the Bridge Company rapidly settled the dispute.

Wellington Cottage, now named Ardara, was built for the Meadows family in the early 1800s. In a stained-glass fanlight over the door is a rising Phoenix, surmounting the initials A.M. for Arthur Meadows. Part of the gardens, including the gatehouse and entrance, were sold for the building of Clifton. It was built by Mrs Mary O'Connor for Thomas O'Reilly. On the remainder of the property down to Fort View, Mrs O'Connor built Glena Terrace.

Beside Ardara stood a large house that was the residence of the Stathams. It became the Rectory about the middle of the nineteenth century and was occupied by Revd Elgee, brother of Lady Wilde (who was also known as Sperenza). It remained the Rectory until 1950, when Mr J.J. Stafford purchased it, together with its garden and the slob bordering it along the Redmond Road. The house was divided into flats for the senior staff of the Fine Wool Fabrics factory. The garden and slob were levelled to form the Timber Yard. The area has since been completely redeveloped.

Richmond House, later the central block of the Loreto Convent, was built for the Duke of Richmond in 1792 but he only lived here for a few months. It was built by Mr White, the son of the founder of White's Hotel. Alderman John Green then lived there. The Loreto Nuns moved here in the summer of 1886. In an article on the Parish of Wexford we find, 'In 1866, Mother Aloysia Sweetman of Gorey sent a foundation to Wexford, and the Nuns obtained a fine residence at Richmond House, Spawell Road, which was dedicated to Our Lady of the Angels.'

Ardruagh was built in the 1890s by Mrs Mary O'Connor (1837-1927), contractor, for Mr Ennis, a local timber merchant and Justice of the Peace, reputedly citing a Norwegian villa spotted during a business trip as a point of influence or reference.

Mr Eakins built Richmond Terrace. It dates from the mid-nineteenth century.

Rockfield House was one of the town houses of the Nunn family. At the request of the Bishop and with the assistance of Richard Devereux, Rockfield House became the convent of the Sisters of Marie Reparatrix in 1870. In the beginning Perpetual Adoration of the Eucharist was not practiced by the sisters, despite the Bishop's wishes. In October 1874 a convent of Perpetual Adoration was established, which most of the original Nuns then entered. The twenty-four hour adoration of the Blessed Sacrament began on 1 January 1875, although Papal approval did not arrive until August of that year. The Nuns only then adopted the distinctive red and white habit. The sisters moved to a convent adjoining the church of the Assumption on 1 May 1887. The St John of God Nuns had their novitiate here until it became a retreat house known as Bethany House. It has since been redeveloped along with surrounding land.

Mr Thomas Pettigrew of Farnogue House built Lorne Ville at the junction of Stoneybatter Road (also known as Poor House or Hospital Road). He also built Farnogue Terrace. It was for a time the residence of Mr Archer. Mrs Cornack of Cromwell's Fort also lived here.

Mr Sinnott built the two houses of Tivoli Terrace. In 1850 Revd Chancellor Hazely transferred the Rectory to Tivoli Terrace. It remained here until the 1970s.

Strandfield was once the residence of James Barry Farrell, County Surveyor. After this it was the residence of the Bradish Family. The gardens of Strandfield, down to the old shore marsh, were laid out as a garden of marshy ponds surrounded by trees.

Riversfield was the residence of Mr Barrington, a merchant. Later it was the residence of Mr Harper, then Mr Wm M. Corcoran of the *Free Press* newspaper and later Mr Tom Ryan.

Carcur House was the residence of the Turner Family and, during the last quarter of the nineteenth century, that of Mr Huggard, solicitor.

On the west side of the road there are two striking cottages that were reputedly built for Captain Peter Codd on very difficult sites by Mr Thomas Willis in the 1840s.

In Griffith's Valuation we find that landowners on Spawell Road include: John E. Redmond; William Walpole; Timothy Gaffney; Ludford Daniel; reps of Charles Jacob; Lady Geary; John Whitcroft; Walter Eakin; Ecclesiastical Commissioners; Nicholas Scallan; reps of Robert John; reps of Henry E. Harvey, and Revd Hugh G. Rhodes.

The Ecclesiastical Commissioners owned the land on which the rectory stood. There were also mentions of a malthouse, a kiln and a forge.

People and Events

Brewers listed in 1824 included Lar Scallan of Spawell.

Richard and John Thomas Devereux attended Behan's school in George Street and later the Protestant Diocesan School in Spawell Road.

Edward Solly Flood notes his diary for 13 March 1894, 'Drove to Wexford in the afternoon, the hotel was crammed with people coming from the North Slob Coursing Meeting and I was hard set to get a bit to eat. Went to club for a couple of hours.' The club in question was the County Wexford Club at Spawell Road, where Edward was a committee member and usually prepared the annual accounts.

St Bridget's Home was used to house flu victims in 1918.

Other

Redmond Park is named for Major Wm Redmond and opened in May 1931.

The building that was Scallan's Brewery back in 1824 later became Rowe's Flour Mill, and was commonly called Spawell Mill. Howard Rowe was Mayor of Wexford in 1911 and he closed Spawell Mill to unions. The building became Redmond Hall, a dance venue, in the 1900s. It was billed as Wexford's Luxury Ballroom in July 1955. Frank and Peggy Spencer of BBC *Come Dancing* fame judged a ballroom dancing competition there. AWL Cash and Carry was located here in 1963.

The lake in the Park was once the Millpond. It was divided into two parts. The smaller part is much earlier and the larger was embanked in about the middle of the nineteenth century by Mr Tom Rowe. The two islands and peninsulas at either end are the remains of the older embankment. The mill was originally worked by a water wheel, but in the mid-nineteenth century a steam engine was installed. The pond was always a favourite playground of children.

In 1917 the Corporation met a delegation from the Wexford Urban Technical Instruction Committee, which included Howard Rowe, Venerable Archdeacon Latham DD, J.S. Thompson, and Mr Lousley (Principal). The purpose of the meeting was to get approval for the use of new premises at Spawell Road. These premises, originally two houses and some land previously occupied by Dr O'Connor, Mr Elgee and the Lawn Tennis Club, would replace the old school building at North Main Street. It was said that the Main Street building was now too small for the 240 students and a reduction in classes would mean the loss of grants. It was agreed that the new premises were a bargain at £750, but some members were worried about the location. They wondered how students from the far end of town would manage. The delegation reported that they had tried to purchase Rossiter's Hardware and Brien & Keatings on the Main Street, but to no avail. In the end it was decided that the 'walk from Maudlintown would do no harm'.

During the 1700s there was a mill in the region of Ardruagh, drawing its water from Farnogue River. The water passed through conduits to supply Richmond Pond and Mill, then underground beneath the stable yard to the Infirmary, across Hill Street and down the hill to the old Ship Channel. After the reclamation, it was piped under the railway embankment to the Slaney. In 1873 the railway rented the water rights of the mill from Mr Harvey at £19 per annum 'while grass grows and water runs'. In around 1925, the railway changed over to the town water supply, but when they tried to terminate their lease on the Mill Stream they found that their solicitors had done too good a job – the lease stands.

In the early 1900s, two concrete paths were laid along Spawell Road. This road, together with the Stoneybatter, Park, Carrig and Redmond Roads were popular walks for the young people of the town. It is said that an accordion player often accompanied the walkers on summer evenings.

Summerhill

Origins and Meaning
Summerhill was a name commonly given to hills that were mostly only usable in fine or summer weather.

Earliest Mentions
In 1809 a Sheriff's Sale of property included land in Summerhill with a dwelling house, according to the *Wexford Herald*.

Buildings
St Mary's has origins dating back to an earlier counterpart known as South Hill. The house was rebuilt for Revd James Browne, Bishop of Ferns. It is the earliest-surviving purpose-built Bishop's palace in the diocese. It has connections with the Stafford and Nolan families, following the relocation of the palace to an adjacent site, reputedly to take advantage of a more picturesque view of Wexford

Harbour. As Stafford's residence it had a double marquee erected in the grounds for a wedding reception in 1961.

The 'Bishop's House' was built as Summerhill House for the Devereux family in the late 1700s. It was redeveloped in the mid to late nineteenth century to designs reputedly prepared by Joseph Aloysius Hansom or Charles Francis Hansom.

St Peter's College, which was opened in 1819, in a three-storey over-raised-basement house, built in 1790.

People and Events

In 1820 a bequest of Walter Redmond was used to establish the Redmond Talbot Orphanage at Summerhill.

Mrs De Rinzy, wife of the clerk of the Grand Jury, died of cholera in 1832 at St Mary's (then South Hill).

The Mercy Nuns, who were introduced to Wexford by Bishop Keating, took over the Redmond Talbot Orphanage at Summerhill in 1842.

Spouts for the provision of drinking water were introduced in the mid-1850s at Green Street, the Folly and Summerhill.

In the census of 1871 there were fifty-seven people recorded in St Michael's Industrial School at Summerhill.

Other

When a new school was mooted for Georges Street it was stated, 'the Mercy School was situated at Summerhill outside the town and was poorly attended especially in bad weather. It was also a very great distance for junior pupils.'

Talbot Street

Origins and Meaning

Talbot Street was built on land owned by James Talbot.

It was also known as Bannister Terrace around 1880.

The name Talbot Street was changed to Pearse Street in 1920 but a plebiscite of 1932 failed to ratify this.

Talbot Green, which is the name that is generally now in use, is a hybrid. The residents combined the names of Talbot Street and Green Street, on which sites the estate was built.

Earliest Mentions

A wide area at the Talbot Street–Green Street junction was known as Slippery Green.

Buildings

Talbot Street had sixty-one inhabited houses and five uninhabited in 1901.

In Griffith's Valuation landowners here include: reps of James Talbot; John Walsh; Patrick Murphy; John Breen; Margaret Madden; Esther Codd; William Doogan [*sic*]; Edward Byrne; Tobias Rossiter; William Byrne, and John Sheffield.

There was a house and forge occupied by William Byrne.

People and Events

A pig was stolen from Mr Connick of Slippery Green in 1808. He said he needed the animal to pay his rent.

Mr Redmond, an employee of Bishopswater Distillery, having been drinking at a public house at Slippery Green, fell down stairs and fractured his skull. He died at Infirmary in 1831, according to the *Wexford Independent*.

Richard Murphy and John Tyghe of Talbot Street were fined 5s each for fighting in a public street in 1902.

In August 1914 some boys from Talbot Street discovered a skull and bones embedded in the sand at Ferrybank. The constable deduced that it had been

Talbot Street was probably preparing for the Eucharistic Congress of 1932 in this picture.

washed in years ago. As the remains could not be identified they were buried at the Workhouse Burial Ground.

In October 1922, four local members of the National Army were killed by a bomb that was dropped on their car from the Railway Bridge at Ferrycarrig. The dead soldiers were from Coolcotts, Talbot Street, Hill Street and Broadway (a village about ten miles south of the town).

In 1951 the County Carnival was held at Byrne's Field. The field, now covered by part of Talbot Green, was a popular location for the regular carnivals of the era.

Temperance Row

Origins and Meaning
Temperance Row is named after a Temperance Hall built here in the 1800s.

The area was called Hey Bey (often written Hai Bai) on a nineteenth-century map. One fanciful explanation for this name was, 'The name is believed to have derived from the bleating of sheep, which were penned here overnight before being sold.'

The street is shown as Selskar Street on the map of 1800 at a time when Abbey Street had the same name.

On a later map, Temperance Row is a street following the boundary wall of Selskar Abbey to its gate in Abbey Street.

Earliest Mentions
This was called Le Cowstrette on a map dated 1540, and later Cowgate Street and Cow Street.

Buildings
Fr Gaul's club was founded in 1933 in a former forge.

Between Selskar Avenue and Well Lane was a row of about eight or ten houses, now demolished.

In Griffith's Valuation we find the land here was owned by: John A. Hogan; Matthew Dodd; John Guilfoyle; James Clancy; Ellen Hayes; Mary Redmond; Maria Kellett, and Nicholas Sinnott.

St Selskar Temperance Society occupied the hall and yard. Matthew Dodd had a workshop and Thomas Roche occupied a forge. Lodgers were noted to be 'occupying rooms over archway'.

In *Sights & Scenes* we read, 'A Temperance Hall, which has latterly been used as a

Temperance Row. This picture shows the Temperance Hall that gave the street its name, to the right behind the cyclist. (*Dominic Kiernan Collection.*)

Temperance Row, showing some of the houses lost to development in the last century. (*Dominic Kiernan Collection.*)

lecture hall for the Mechanics' Institute, was erected immediately adjoining the northern boundary wall of the churchyard of the abbey, subsequent to the visit of the great apostle of the Temperance cause, the Very Revd Father Mathew, in 1835.'

People and Events

Fr Mathew was in Wexford on 8 April 1840. A crusade began at the Friary on 10 April 1841 and thousands attended. The Temperance Society was started at Clancy's Hote, in Anne Street in 1850. Thomas Darcy McGee was the first secretary. There were societies at Selskar, Francis Street and the Faythe. A Temperance Hall was built at Selskar. There the newspapers were read aloud to benefit those unable to read. This practice was also beneficial as newspapers were scarce.

Walter Connors, locksmith, Westgate, owned some of the land.

The Wexford GAA Club met in the Temperance Hall in 1887.

Wexford Corporation acquired three houses here in the early 1960s.

Other

Dodd's Lane was on the north side of Temperance Row, opposite Dodd's Coachbuilders. In one of the houses on Dodd's Lane lived Mrs Singleton, who sold herrings from a basket. She travelled the streets calling, 'Fresh Rosslares, fresh Rosslares.' The herrings cost 2*d*, 3*d* or 6*d* a dozen, depending on supply.

The Old Pound (later St Peter's Square)

Origins and Meaning

The Old Pound takes its name from the animal pound located there. Cattle were impounded in livery stables while awaiting shipment.

The later name of St Peter's Square is associated with St Peter's church, which in turn was associated with St Peter's Gate, one of the original entrances to the walled town.

The remains of St Peter's church were removed in 1897 by an improving Corporation in order to create St Peter's Square.

Earliest Mentions

Cardinal Rinucinni celebrated Mass in St Peter's church when he visited Wexford in 1647.

In Pigot's Directory of 1820 the Old Pound is listed as one of the Wexford streets.

In *Sights & Scenes* it is noted:

> At the Old Pound are the remains of an ancient church dedicated to St Peter. Several large stones, which constituted portions of the foundation, appear protruding above the mound of earth, which occupies the comparatively extensive area, which is bounded on the south by a small stream, on the east by the ancient town-wall, and on the north and west by large stores and dwelling houses.

The following advertisement appeared in the *Wexford Independent* on 21 November 1838:

> By the particular desires of the graziers of Forth and Bargy and surrounding baronies, and the buyers of stock from Waterford, Ross and Enniscorthy, sellers are asked to show their cattle on each Saturday at the old-established pig market in the Old Pound, as being the best place calculated for the sale of stock in this town.

Buildings

A malthouse and dwelling house at the Old Pound, in possession of Philip Walsh, was to let in 1817. Applications were to be by letter to Vigors Harvey Esq. (post paid), Hammerton Hall, York, or Henry Archer, Ballyseskin, according to an advertisement in the *Wexford Herald*.

The row of houses on the south side of the Old Pound (or St Peter's Square) date from the 1870s.

Thomas Doyle, builder and carpenter, had an address at Erin Cottage in 1888.

In Griffith's Valuation the Old Pound is listed as having two malthouses with kilns. The landowners include: Mary Furlong; Richard Walsh; Charles J.V. Harvey, and Sir William Geary.

People and Events

Thomas Browne (1757-1838) lived in Old Pound House. He owned two malthouses. He was sentenced to death with Grogan in 1798 but was reprieved.

In 1824, Philip Walsh was listed as a brewer at the Old Pound.

In 1843, James Clancy, painter, was listed at the Old Pound.

William Boggan of the Old Pound was noted as shipmaster of the vessel *Onward*, in a list dating from 1864.

Charles Stewart Parnell made a speech from the steps of the present Seskin House in St Peter's Square in October 1881.

A pig market operated at the Old Pound in 1883.

In 1887 Kelly's auction yard was at the Old Pound.

The Old Pound, showing the site of the pound (noted by white walls) across the square. (*Dominic Kiernan Collection.*)

It was suggested as the site for a park in 1897.

In October 1888 it was reported in a newspaper that land in other parts of the town was mortgaged by Wexford Corporation to raise the £2,500 needed to build twenty-six labourers' dwellings at the Old Pound. These were most probably the houses of Roche's Terrace.

Polling in the Municipal elections of 1903 took place at 'The Tholsel and the national schools at the Old Pound between 8a.m. and 8p.m'. The school was on Roche's Road.

The St Patrick's Day parade in 1914 assembled at St Peter's Square. At 2p.m. sharp the Mayor arrived, in chains of office and robes, attended by his civic officers in their attractive regalia. His Worship was accompanied in his carriage by 'Wexford's Grand Old Man' Ben Hughes.

In 1914, when the Scottish Borderers fired on the crowds in Dublin, massive numbers joined the Volunteers, including 200 foundry workers who marched from St Peter's Square to the Park. Two full companies marched to Edenvale in July 1914. They were met at Fahey's Cross by the Castlebridge Corps and were addressed by Fr James Quigley, PP, at the Reading Rooms. An impromptu céilí was held at Edenvale. They returned via Crossabeg and Ferrycarrig, before disbanding at the Old Pound. In September 1914, 1,200 Volunteers met at the park.

The square was a popular venue for rallies over the years.

On 21 April 1918, the Old Pound was the scene of an anti-conscription protest. Revd Mark O'Byrne, Fr Ryan, Richard Corish, James Sinnott and J.J. Stafford addressed a crowd of over 5,000.

Also in 1918, Fr O'Flanagan, vice-president of Sinn Féin, addressed a meeting at St Peter's Square, in support of local Dáil candidate Mr Jim Ryan. Fights erupted during the speeches between rival groups, and the RIC baton-charged the crowd. At the conclusion of the meeting the square was cordoned off by police and the Sinn Féin supporters were only allowed to leave via Peter's Street, with an escort. Scuffles continued in the town throughout the evening.

On Sunday 9 April 1922, Michael Collins spoke to a record crowd in St Peter's Square, who applauded the treaty. Collins was presented with a set of pipes.

A hire car was available from J.J. Bell of the Old Pound in 1922. In the same year John Sinnott & Co. announced the opening of a workshop at St Peter's Square for cabinet-making and funeral undertaking.

In 1941 the Corporation advertised for tenders for the construction of air-raid shelters. Each was to accommodate fifty people and they were to be located as follows: one at Cornmarket; two at the Town Hall, also in Cornmarket; two at the New Market in the Bullring; one at Selskar; one at Patrick's Square; four at St Peter's Square; two at King Street, and one at the Crescent.

During the Wexford celebrations for the inauguration of the Irish Republic in 1949, the tricolour flew half-mast at St Peter's Square. Brendan Corish TD read the 1916 Proclamation and three volleys were fired by the FCA.

Cousins Ltd of the Old Pound still operated a bottling plant in 1966.

Other

The Deddery stretched under the present Garda station from St Peter's Square. It was named after the mortuary of St Peter's church, which stood here. A cavern or vault was uncovered there in the 1890s and bones found were re-interred at Crosstown.

In around 1840, there were as many as 250 men and women employed in the hatting trade in Wexford. The principal employees at the time were Mr Corish, Mr Archer, Mr Peter Sinnott, Mr William Jeffares, and Mr Thomas Jefferies, who lived in Mr P. Hynes's drapery shop in the Bullring. They employed thirty to forty men each. Mr Sinnott also had a branch workshop in Clongeen. In addition, there were a number of small manufacturers who worked with their own families, and employed two to six men. These included: Mr Hynes, John Street; Mr Burke, Laffan's Lane; Messrs Whitmore and Jones, Church Lane, and Mr Gurley of Old Pound.

Trinity Street

Origins and Meaning

The street takes its name from the ancient church of the Holy Trinity.

The church of the Holy Trinity was situated on the slope of the Danish knoll at the foot of the castle. 'The women of the seventeenth century had great reverence for this church and came in solemn procession, the oldest first and the others following. They make three turns round the ruins and repeat the ceremony many times.' This devotion could last three or four hours.

Earliest Mentions

It is not noted on Lewis's 1831 map.

It is noted on the 1840 map.

Trinity Street appears in Griffith's map.

Buildings

Mrs Fanning owned houses at Trinity Street in 1889.

The bacon factory opened in around 1885, later becoming Clover Meats.

Star Works, owned by the Hearne family, was sited to the south of the South Station on the seaward side of the railway line. It opened in the 1890s.

Trinity Street had forty houses in the census of 1901, with thirty-four inhabited and six uninhabited.

The Talbot Hotel was originally the home of Mary O'Connor. She operated a school there in 1858. It later became a public house and finally a hotel, with the ship wharf of the Liverpool Steamship conveniently situated opposite, behind the current apartment block. When the Nationalist leader Countess Markievicz visited Wexford early in 1919, a crowd of over 2,000 met her at Carcur and they paraded through Wexford to the Talbot Hotel. Many tricolours were in evidence. Accounts of such events were subject to official censorship, even in the local newspapers of the time. The Talbot Hotel also provided breakfast for the flooded out residents of the King Street area in 1947.

But it was not all war and want. Wexford's 'Miss Hot Pants' of 1971 was chosen at the Talbot Hotel, winning a holiday in Butlins. Among the top-line entertainers appearing at the Talbot during the swinging sixties were Marianne Faithful, Joseph Locke, Marmalade, The Troggs and Billy Fury. Then, in the 1970s, the ballad sessions on a Saturday night with McMurrough were legendary for the crowds, the craic and the ceol.

James Furniss of Anne Street founded the gasworks in 1830, with its plant at Trinity Street.

The house named Dubross was that of the manager of the gasworks. It was built around 1865.

The Earl of Mulgrave visited Wexford in 1836. Cannon were set up on the quays for a salute, and he arrived at the Courthouse at 4p.m. with a company of Hussars. The parade went along the quay, past the gasworks, up the New Road to the Faythe, and back to Main Street.

The original gasworks went bankrupt in 1865 and a new company, Wexford Gas Consumers Limited, was founded. A letter was received by the Wexford Harbour Commissioners from the Wexford Gas Company in 1916 to say, 'The Commissioners at the present time owe £71 5s 1d for two quarters gas and a third will soon fall due and we will have to put out the lights on the quay on 1 April, unless payment is received in the meantime.'

The letter was forwarded to the Corporation for payment due to the depleted funds of the Board. The town was plunged into darkness in 1918 by a strike at the Gasworks. While in digs in George Street in the early 1950s, a local recalls that lighting was by gas. Wexford Gas Consumers Company ceased operation on 4 September 1990.

Wexford Town Railway Station (South) opened here in 1886 and closed in 1977. The office of the manager of the Irish section of Fishguard and Rosslare Railways and Harbours Company was located there. The South Station was actually more impressive than the North. Here, the Rosslare-bound train arrived on the seaward platform and the 'up train' went to the landside. Hundreds of people crowded on to the platform each fine Sunday. There were tee-shirts, khaki short pants, flowery

Trinity Street, when the gasworks dominated. (*O'Connor Collection.*)

dresses, straw hats, flat caps, cardigans, pullovers and plastic macs to beat the band. Youngsters amused themselves by 'pegging' stones into the water of the harbour just feet away. Daredevils crossed the tracks and sat on the harbour wall. The ladies crowded into the little waiting room with its bench, ticket office and pot-bellied stove. Heads craned out over the platform edge. In the days of steam they watched for the plume of smoke as the train approached the quay.

In Griffith's Valuation we find that unsurprisingly John E. Redmond is the principal landowner. Others include William Maguire and Mary Byrne.

The old dockyard was vacant but the sheds and packet wharf were in operation. Mr Furniss held a lease on the gasworks, Johanna Codd had a coal yard and John Furlong had a forge.

People and Events

At the southern end of the quay in 1832 Redmond established his dockyard. The first vessel built here was *The Vulcan*, for a local ship owner called Nathaniel Hughes. It was launched in 1833. The dockyard employed 100 men at its peak and was responsible for building schooners and barques up to 360 tons. To provide access to his shipyard Redmond built Trinity Street, which connected New Street, now Parnell Street, with the quay. The *Antelope* was the last schooner to be built at this yard. Lewis remarks, 'Shipping interests have been materially promoted by the construction of a patent slip and shipbuilding yard at the southern end of his embankment, from which a vessel of 70 tons has already been launched. Vessels belonging to the port had previously been built at Milford and Liverpool.'

In 1902 Edward Berry of Folly Lane was charged with stealing lead from Wexford Gas Company and was sentenced to three months with hard labour.

On Thursday 10 January 1912, two wagonloads of beds were moved from the South Station to Brien & Keating's public house on Main Street. The premises had been acquired by Pierce's for conversion into a hostel for sixty blacklegs, who were expected to arrive in Wexford.

A woman was brought to court in 1917 for stealing coal from the quayside. This was the property of the Wexford Gas Consumers Company and was picked up from around the carts as they were being loaded. The constable said that she had a half stone of coal in her bag, although she had been warned not to take it. It was stated in her defence that such scavenging was a long-standing practice on the quays and there had not been prosecutions before. The justice decided to be lenient in dealing with the case but warned that such a tradition should be ended.

The Second World War was known as the Emergency in Ireland. The Local Defence Force of volunteers drilled at the Talbot car park two nights per week, under Ned Lacey of John Street and Willie Flush from Trinity Street, both ex-British Army.

The Star Engineering Works, one of the Lockout Foundries, became an assembly plant for Renault cars, and the first Wexford-assembled Renault 8 drove through the factory gates on Tuesday 23 November 1965.

Other

Trinity Place, a lane off Trinity Street, is known locally as Matty's Alley.

Emmett Place, another lane off Trinity Street, was built with fifteen houses in 1897. Wexford Corporation built a handball alley there in 1957 with space for 300 supporters, to commemorate Robert Emmett (1778-1803).

In 1914 a special committee of Wexford Corporation reported on the unsatisfactory service being rendered by the gas company:

> The committee appointed a cyclist as a temporary gas inspector to prove the complaints. He (Mr N.J. Cosgrave) started his rounds at nightfall and recorded lamps not lit or not giving sufficient light. On one night he found forty-seven lamps unlighted and eleven defective. The gas company replied that the Corporation could employ a person to light the lamps with gas being supplied from them along with automatic lighting arrangements. After much discussion the Corporation and gas company agreed to each pay half of the 14s wages of the gas inspector for a trial period.

Waterloo Road

Origins and Meaning

Waterloo Road is named after the Battle of Waterloo.

Prior to 1815 it was Methodist Row.

The name was changed to McCurtain Street in 1920 but the change was not upheld in the 1932 plebiscite.

Earliest Mentions

The road is noted but not named in the map of 1800.

It is noted as Methodist Row in 1812.

It was called Waterloo Place in 1840.

Buildings

The big houses on the south side of the street are believed to have been constructed between 1815 and 1840, and may originally have been war veterans' or Royal Irish Constabulary officers' houses.

In 1838 St Aidan's on Waterloo Road was established by Revd Myles Murphy or Revd James Keating, Bishop of Ferns, as the Presbytery for the Roman Catholic

Waterloo Road, showing the walls of the Presentation Convent School on the left with some pupils outside. The flash of light there denotes the narrow entrance gate. (*Dominic Kiernan Collection.*)

clergy. One of its residents was Fr James Roche, the power behind the building of the twin churches.

The schools of the Presentation Order were located at Waterloo Road, taking boys from junior infants to first class and girls from junior infants to Leaving Certificate.

Wexford Corporation provided two houses in 1950 to house specialist workers at the Fine Wool Fabrics factory in Drinagh.

Griffith's Valuation shows the landowners here as: reps of James Percival; Thomas Redmond; Walter Redmond; James Atkin; Catherine Lacey; Walter Eakin; Marianne Ward; James Kinsella; Margaret Moran; Hannah Myers; Thomas Cullen, and Revd Lawrence Kirwan.

People and Events
In December 1947 there was major flooding at Waterloo Road and TD Sinnott had people from the area invited to his house at Clonard.

Other
Residents of Corry's Villas requested a name change to Waterloo Road West in 1953.

Paradise Row was home to the family of Thomas D'Arcy Magee, who was to find fame in Canada in the 1800s. Canadian tourists wishing to find the homestead are not in for much luck. The remains of Paradise Row are under weeds and briars between the houses of Waterloo Road and Corry's Villas, going down to the Presentation sports field.

Westgate

Note:We will use the delineation of the Griffith map in this street to decide that Spawell Road starts at the old town wall.

Origins and Meaning

Westgate takes its name from one of the gates of the town wall. Until recent years it was assumed that the existing gate visible in the adjoining yard was the west gate. This has since been disproved.

Westgate was also called Cow Gate. The original gate and tower were built in 1300 by Sir Stephen Devereux and last used in 1828.

Earliest Mentions

Weststreete (Westgate) was one of Wexford's suburbs in 1659.

It is called Westgate Street in Griffith's.

Buildings

West Gate House, originally dating from about 1825, was the town house of De Rinzy of Clobemon Hall, near Bunclody. The De Rinzys were the subject of a poem called 'The Doom of De Rinzy', by Thomas Furlong of Scarawalsh.

Local tradition recalls houses lining the south side of the lane, where the current restaurant (earlier the Old Granary and formerly Nunn's Grain Stores dating from the late 1800s) now stands. Previously, the gradient of the lane was so steep that carts could only haul up half loads at a time.

In Griffith's Valuation we find landowners in Westgate include: William Kellett; reps of William Clifford; John Richards; John A. Hogan; Revd Richard W. Elgee; Richard McDonnell; Walter O'Connor, and Matthew Dodd.

People and Events

Capt. Cullen, barrack master, lived here in 1824. Ground-floor recesses were for toll collectors, with a lock-up and guard room above.

In 1826 Sarah Cullen had a school here charging fees of 3½d per week and attracting eighteen pupils.

Other

Kaat's shipyard once dominated the Westgate. Van Kaat came from the Netherlands around 1641 to establish shipbuilding near Westgate, where the waters of the river ran along the shore. He built ships for the Irish Confederate Navy. Anthony Van Kaat was transported to Barbados in 1650s.

William Street

Origins and Meaning

William Street is possibly named for King William.

It was renamed James Connolly Street in 1920 but again the residents failed to agree in 1932 and the old name persists. The new name might have been appropriate as Connolly stayed with Richard Corish in William Street when he visited Wexford during the 1911 Lockout.

Earliest Mentions

William Street does not exist on the map of 1831.

On 18 May 1833 a notice was published, 'Improvements proceeding on quay, beyond Crescent, line extends beyond Mr White's Castle as far as Fishers Row. A road is to be formed to the quay, to give entry to the people from Forth and Bargy.'

It was open by 1836 for the Viceroy's parade.

Buildings

In the census of 1901 William Street had fifty-three houses listed, with fifty inhabited and three uninhabited.

Twelve houses were built in 1904.

The small row of gated houses in the middle of the street is Lambert Terrace.

No.35 was the home of Richard Corish, who was elected mayor of Wexford in 1920 and held the position for twenty-five consecutive years until his death in 1945.

There was a shed at the corner of the present Fishers Row owned by Frank Swan, and the big house on the corner was Donnelley's.

Griffith's Valuation shows ownership in this street to include: Mary Walsh; Mary Hobbs and Editha Hatchell; Elizabeth Rackard; Susan Hughes; Henry Mulligan; James Morris; George Murphy; Jane Batt; Matthew Tracey; Thomas Neale; Robert Stafford; Patrick Hendrick; Christopher Codd; Thomas Willis; Edward Waters, and Mary Johnston.

People and Events

Capt. Thomas Walsh, known as 'Lannigan', was born in No.3 William Street. He is often described as 'the father of Wexford's sailors'. He was the son of Captain James Walsh, who died of fever onboard the barque *Kate,* of which he was skipper.

Lannigan first went to sea at the age of thirteen and finished his maritime travels at the age of sixty-eight years. He attained his Master Mariner's certificate at the age of twenty-one. His first command was *Rambler*. He sailed as Master

William Street, with a dog resting in the concrete-slabbed roadway and a lady walking a toddler past some houses with window shutters. (*Dominic Kiernan Collection.*)

William Street towards Trinity Street and the quays. The gasworks are prominent in the distant centre. (*Dominic Kiernan Collection.*)

on fifty-three vessels and never lost a ship. Captain Walsh was the holder of the coveted Square-rigged Master's certificate. At one time he was a commander in the Wexford fleet of sailing ships known as the 'Galatzmen', whose epic races home from the Black Sea with grain and cargoes were as famous in those days as those of the China clippers. He appeared on the front cover of a book of shanties called *Songs of the Wexford Coast*. He was the father of ten sons and three daughters. He had forty-eight grandchildren and fifty-three great grandchildren.

In the Ardcavan tragedy one of the men in charge of the boat was Aleck Swan of William Street. The victims included Mary Furlong, William Street. Mary Furlong, who was known as 'Mossie' by her friends, had just announced her engagement. Her father and mother, a brother and sister and her fiancé had accompanied her to the races. At the subsequent inquest the first witness heard was John Furlong, William Street, a sailor and the father of Mary Furlong.

People in William Street were fined in 1903 for allowing donkeys to wander.

In February 1914 the Corporation discussed difficulties with house numbers. There were three No.4s in William Street.

For houses at William Street in 1939, the cost of the Gas Company piping for six lights per house was £1 each after base pipes being laid.

Larry Murphy from William Street was an owner/skipper. His vessel was called the *Express*. It was lost off the Arklow Bank and Larry, his brother Johnny and Myles Furlong died in the tragic incident.

Wygram

Origins and Meaning
Wygram Place at the top of Hill Street, formerly called Breen's Lane, has been an important road junction since the prehistoric Coolcotts track forked here for the Ferry and the Market Place. The Wygram family lived for a short time at nearby Wygram House, and the area was part of the Wygram Estate.

Earliest Mentions
On the 1800 map the road is not named.

The area was built up in a map of 1831.

In 1845 Wygram Place was noted only on the street where Wygram House stands.

In Griffith's there is a notation of Wygram Place going from Hill Street round the corner to the location of the present Davitt Road.

Monument Place is also noted around the Vallotin monument.

Wygram, in the days before motorcars took over. The horse trough beside the monument indicates the importance of horses and donkeys. There are a few cattle down near the corner of Hill Street, possibly on the way to the fair at the end of that street. (*Dominic Kiernan Collection.*)

Buildings

Wygram House, dating from the 1860s, is possibly on the site of an 1820s edifice.

The Municipal Buildings was once Tate (or Tait) School, a mixed school for boarders and day pupils, built with the bequest of a Wexford man who made his fortune in the Jamaica sugar trade. It reopened under new management in October 1941 but on 5 February 1951 it was informally opened as Town Hall.

The building behind the railings, now divided into houses, was a Lying-in Hospital in 1846.

Seven houses were built here in 1904.

Mr Maddocks built the present Gaynor's grocery shop and public house. The house was originally thatched. It later became the property of Walshes. It was here that three famous Wexford people were brought up: the late Mr John (Sandy) Walshe, famous actor of stage and screen; Dr Tom Walshe, founder of the Wexford Opera Festival and for many years its Artistic Director, and Miss Nellie Walshe, Contralto.

In Griffith's Valuation the major landowner is Sir Robert Fitzwygram. Other owners are: John Maddock; Anastasia Sheerin; William Ormonde; Thomas Hanrahan; Thomas Lacey; Nicholas Maddock and Robert Copeland.

The Lying-in Hospital is listed as a house, garden and yard.

Thomas Dempsey occupied a house, office and tan yard.

Wygram, giving an excellent view of the monument and the diverging roads to Newtown Road (to the right) and Windmills Hill (to the left). (*Dominic Kiernan Collection.*)

People and Events

A monument to the memory of Major Vallotin stands at Wygram. The Corporation minutes of 30 September 1793 read,

> It was unanimously voted that a monument be erected in the church in the town, and a monumental obelisk raised on the spot where he was killed at the expense of the Corporation to the memory of the late Major Charles Vallotin of the 69th Regiment of Infantry who fell in defence of the town of Wexford when attacked by a dangerous and riotous mob.

In 1887 the Corporation authorised the expenditure of £20 to enclose the monument.

Mr Nolan of Wygram owned the first wireless set in Wexford. He sent away for the parts and assembled it himself, with the help of a friend. His father refused to loan him a ladder to erect the aerial, saying it was 'nothing but witchcraft'. It met with the disapproval of the clergy of the day.

Other

Monument Place, mentioned in Griffith's Valuation, is part of what we now refer to as Wygram. The name comes from the Vallotin Monument. Charles Hewson owned the collection of six houses and gardens.

Bibliography

Bassett, *Wexford County Guide & Directory* (Dublin 1885)

Colfer, B. – Wexford, a Town and its Landscape, Cork University Press 2008

Enright, Michael – Men of Iron (Wexford 1987)

Griffith, G. – Chronicles of County Wexford (Enniscorthy 1877)

Griffith's Valuation data

Hore, P.H. – History of Town and County of Wexford – 1906 (reprinted Professional Books 1979)

Kehoe, M.T. - Wexford – Its Streets and People – undated

Lacy, T. – Sights and Scenes in Our Fatherland (London 1863)

Ranson, J. – Songs of the Wexford Coast (Wexford 1975)

Reck, P. – Wexford – A Municipal History, Mulgannon Publications, 1987

Roche, Rossiter, Hurley, Hayes – Walk Wexford Ways – 1988

Rossiter, Hurley, Roche, Hayes – A Wexford Miscellany – WHP 1994

Rossiter, N. – Wexford Port – WCTU 1989

Rossiter, N. – My Wexford – Nonsuch 2006

Rossiter, N. – Wexford, a history, a tour, a miscellany – Nonsuch 2005

Newspapers
Wexford People
Wexford Echo
Wexford Independent
Wexford Herald

Journals
Wexford Historical Society – various articles
The Past – various articles

Personal Notes/Unpublished Research
Eamon Doyle
Liam Gaul
Sylvia O'Connor
Jack O'Leary
James Pierce
John E. Sinnott

Websites
http://www.iol.ie/~wexfordways/index.htm
http://www.buildingsofireland.com/